American Enterprise Institute
Studies in Economic Policy

Wage-Price Standards and Economic Policy

Jack A. Meyer

Wage-Price Standards and Economic Policy

Jack A. Meyer

Wage-Price Standards and Economic Policy

Jack A. Meyer

American Enterprise Institute for Public Policy Research
Washington and London

Jack A. Meyer is resident fellow in economics and director of health policy research at the American Enterprise Institute. He is the former assistant director for wage-price monitoring of the U.S. Council on Wage and Price Stability.

Library of Congress Cataloging in Publication Data

Meyer, Jack, 1944-
  Wage-price standards and economic policy.

  (AEI studies ; 358)
  1. Council on Wage and Price Stability (U.S.)—History. 2. Wage-price policy—United States—History. 3. United States—Economic Policy—1971-1981. I Title. II. Series.
HC110.W24M49 1982   339.5'0973   82-8810
ISBN 0-8447-3490-X   AACR2

AEI Studies 358

Printed in the United States of America

Contents

1 INTRODUCTION 1

2 THE DEVELOPMENT OF THE COUNCIL ON 3
WAGE AND PRICE STABILITY

The Initial Concept of CWPS 4
CWPS Activities, 1974–1978 5
Issues in Federal Regulation 13

3 WAGE-PRICE GUIDELINES: AUXILIARY POLICY 16
TOOL OR SELF-STANDING PROGRAM?

Alternative Ways of Viewing Wage-Price
Guidelines 16
Wage Indexation 19
The Carter Guidelines 21
Confusion over the Causes of Inflation 28
An Alternative Conceptual Framework 28

4 WAGE-PRICE GUIDELINES: A CASE OF 32
REGULATORY EXPANSION

Some Arbitrary Distinctions in the Application of
Wage-Price Guidelines 33
The Growing Complexity of Applying Wage-Price
Guidelines 36
Obtaining Compliance through Compromise 39
The Immense Task of Wage-Price Regulation 41
The Need for a Broader Perspective on
Regulatory Effectiveness 43

5   ASSESSING THE EFFECTIVENESS OF THE   46
WAGE–PRICE STANDARDS

    Assessing the Independent Effect of
      the Standards 48
    Interpreting the CWPS Estimates 53
    GAO's Sensitivity Analysis 56
    The Importance of the Postcontrols Period 60

6   INCOMES POLICIES OVER THE PAST TWO DECADES   64

    The Kennedy-Johnson Guideposts 64
    The Nixon Controls 67
    The Interim Period 69
    The Carter Guidelines 74

7   CONCLUSION   77

    APPENDIX   79

Acknowledgments

I am grateful to Patricia Samors for her valuable research assistance. Her contribution was comprehensive, including the compilation and organization of data, the review of literature, and the drafting of chapter 6.

I am deeply indebted to Marvin H. Kosters in two respects. First, he reviewed a preliminary draft of the book and suggested many useful revisions that improved the subsequent draft considerably. Second, through ongoing informal discussions in recent years he has helped to critique, refine, and enhance my understanding of the subject matter covered in this book. Such a contribution is hard to measure, but very important. I appreciate the careful reading of an earlier draft by Sean Sullivan, who provided numerous helpful comments and suggestions. The responsibility for any remaining problems is, of course, mine alone.

I also appreciate the guidance and assistance I received from Carol Treanor and Eduardo Somensatto in my econometric work. And finally, but certainly not least, I thank Gretchen Erhardt for her careful typing and overall organization of this manuscript. Her professional approach to this project both expedited and improved the final product.

1
Introduction

This study assesses the wage-price policy pursued by the U.S. Council on Wage and Price Stability (CWPS) during its six-year existence from 1974 to 1980. Focusing primarily on the wage-price standards introduced by President Carter in 1978, the study evaluates their effect on wage and price trends in the two years during which they were in force.

Chapter 2 traces the development of the Council on Wage and Price Stability and highlights its main functions and accomplishments during the four years (1974–1978) preceding the introduction of formal wage-price standards. From 1975 to 1978, the author worked with the council, and from 1977 to 1978 he served as the council's assistant director for wage and price monitoring. During this period CWPS, a small agency, concentrated primarily on studying selected sectors of the economy and government regulations in an effort to make marginal improvements in the efficiency of the economy. The agency monitored price and wage developments in various sectors of the economy believed to be sources of inflationary pressures, conducted a number of special studies of collective bargaining, industrial capacity, and measures of inflation, and intervened in numerous government rule-making and regulatory proceedings to find more efficient and effective ways of achieving the objectives of federal regulatory policy.

Chapter 3 provides a conceptual framework for analyzing the role of wage-price standards and contrasts three alternative viewpoints on wage-price standards: (1) that they should play an active role as the first line of defense against inflation; (2) that they should have a more passive, supportive role, using wage-price targets as an adjunct to anti-inflationary fiscal and monetary policy; and (3) that wage-price standards have no useful role in economic policy, but constitute a threat to a persistent anti-inflationary macroeconomic policy. In terms of these categories, President Carter's wage-price guidelines are described as an "active" incomes policy, despite some administration claims to the contrary. It is suggested here that the guidelines were intended to be a self-standing anti-inflation program, that they were

1

discredited at the outset, and that instead of being abandoned, they remained in place for two years, with little support from either the public or the administration.

Chapter 4 analyzes the Carter wage-price standards as a case study of government regulation. It describes the contradiction within the Carter administration between its commitment to reduce or simplify government regulation and its introduction of a program that would regulate millions of wage and price decisions. The chapter presents both technical and political criteria for defining the scope of a wage-price program and provides an explanation of the ways in which the initial simplicity of a wage-price program inevitably is lost. Various inequities in the Carter guidelines are highlighted, as are the dangers of bending the rules to accommodate economic units having considerable market power or political power. The chapter ends with a detailed description of the work of CWPS in developing trigger prices[1] for the steel industry, a process that illustrates the monumental task and the inevitable arbitrary decisions facing government agencies trying to set prices in an industry.

Chapter 5 assesses the effectiveness of the wage-price standards by reviewing the evidence from econometric work performed elsewhere and by considering the author's own estimation of wage equations. The results of a sensitivity analysis are used to call into question claims by the Carter administration that the guidelines had a noticeable effect on the pace of wage increases. The program effect claimed by CWPS is shown to evaporate in the face of slight changes in the specification or measurement of the independent variables and with the inclusion of a year of postcontrols experience in the analysis.

Chapter 6 contains a brief history of the last three U.S. experiences with incomes policies — the Kennedy-Johnson guideposts, the Nixon controls, and the Carter guidelines. Chapter 7 presents the author's conclusions.

---

[1] The trigger price mechanism was designed to expedite and simplify investigations of alleged dumping by foreign steel producers and was intended to be a substitute for lengthy formal procedures specified by the trade statutes. CWPS calculated trigger prices for dozens of categories of steel by estimating cost differentials attributable to various products.

2

The Development of the Council on Wage and Price Stability

In his first presidential address to Congress on August 12, 1974, President Ford asked Congress to reactivate the Cost of Living Council to deal with inflation. The president stated his opposition to controls and urged Congress to create an agency that would "monitor wages and prices to expose abuses."[1] On August 15 the Senate Committee on Banking, Housing, and Urban Affairs held hearings and forwarded S. 3919 to the full House. This bill was passed by the Senate on August 19 and by the House on August 20. On August 24 President Ford signed the bill,[2] and the Council on Wage and Price Stability (CWPS) was created.

There were several manifestations of congressional caution in this act, reflecting the concern of both the legislative and the executive branches that a monitoring agency could evolve into a controls agency. First, the council was explicitly forbidden to reimpose controls and was given no authority to limit or delay wage and price increases. Second, CWPS was given a short life, as the act would be terminated on August 15, 1975, giving Congress a year to reconsider the need for a monitoring agency. Third, CWPS was not given the power to subpoena data from firms or unions during its first year.[3]

Although the formal powers of CWPS were quite limited, its mandate was broad, directing the agency to examine wage and price behavior throughout the economy and to ascertain the extent to which the activities of the federal government were contributing to inflation.

[1] See Gerald R. Ford, presidential address to the Congress, August 12, 1974.
[2] P.L. 93-387, reprinted in Allendex, along with the statement of President Ford on August 24, 1974.
[3] See Council on Wage and Price Stability Act. In August 1975, Congress gave CWPS the power to issue subpoenas for the attendance and testimony of witnesses at hearings and the production of books, papers, and documents by entities whose annual gross revenues exceeded $5 million. (See P.L. 93-387, as amended by P.L. 94-78.) At this time CWPS was also granted the power to require periodic reports for the submission of information maintained in the ordinary course of business.

Although the inflationary impact of government policies had been reviewed on an ad hoc basis in connection with earlier wage-price programs, the new act marked the first time that the federal government turned the anti-inflation spotlight on itself in a systematic fashion.

The CWPS mandate included directives to review and analyze industrial capacity, demand, supply, and the effect of economic concentration and anticompetitive practices; work with labor and management to improve the structure of collective bargaining; improve wage and price data bases; review and appraise the various programs, policies, and activities of federal departments and agencies to assess their inflationary impact; and intervene in rule-making, rate-making, and licensing proceedings before federal departments and agencies to present its views of the potential inflationary impact of the possible outcomes of such proceedings.[4]

The Initial Concept of CWPS

As initially conceived, CWPS was an agency charged with digging beneath the surface of inflationary trends within individual sectors of the economy and with detecting inflationary pressures emanating from the actions of federal agencies. It was not charged with developing an anti-inflation policy, but rather was envisioned as a group of troubleshooters who would probe for anticompetitive behavior underlying industry price trends, structural characteristics of collective bargaining believed to inflate wages, and cost-increasing aspects of federal rules and regulations. CWPS was given a decidedly microeconomic focus, and its activities were viewed as an adjunct or supplement to the development of appropriate fiscal and monetary policies which were clearly intended to be the first line of defense against inflation.

Although the functional role of CWPS was carefully restricted, the scope of its activities was comprehensive. While the agency lacked "teeth," it was free to explore cost-increasing pressures from the farm to the factory and from truck regulations issued by the Interstate Commerce Commission (ICC) to safety rules promulgated by the Occupational Safety and Health Administration (OSHA).

The Role of CWPS. The position of the Council on Wage and Price Stability was somewhere between that of an intragovernmental microeconomic monitoring agency and an independent agency at arm's

---

[4] Council on Wage and Price Stability Act, P.L. 93-387.

4

length from the administration. It seems accurate to describe CWPS, at least during the 1974–1978 period, as a quasi-independent agency with some margin for independent maneuver, though not having the degree of independence exercised by an agency such as the ICC.

Its ambiguous status presented both problems and opportunities for CWPS. The problems occurred when firms, unions, or agencies whose activities were being monitored by CWPS were unsure of the extent to which the agency had administration backing and should be taken seriously. The opportunities involved the White House's option of using CWPS to influence wage-price behavior without overt presidential involvement.

In this early period the White House could speak *through* CWPS, but CWPS could also speak *to* the White House. The president could express concern through the agency over particular price and wage actions, and CWPS could in turn prod the Executive Office from within to cause the government to change its own cost-increasing policies.

Although it is difficult to ascertain how well this two-way street really worked, there were numerous instances in which the council's price monitoring and jawboning efforts appeared to have the tacit blessing, but not the overt sanction, of top administration officials.

This was particularly apparent in cases of major steel and automobile price increases receiving considerable media attention. Such increases create a dilemma for an administration. On the one hand, there is a desire to avoid a confrontation with business, coupled (sometimes) with an awareness of the dangers of government meddling in business decision making. On the other hand, there is often a perceived political need to "do something" in response to a very visible price increase. The role played by CWPS in price monitoring, studies of industry, and occasional jawboning could be viewed as a way out of this dilemma. The council's activities reflected a concern over inflation, but insofar as there was uncertainty over the administration's official endorsement of these activities, CWPS could act as a buffer, insulating the Executive Office from overt involvement in wage-price policy.

CWPS Activities, 1974–1978

The types of activities conducted by the CWPS staff can be divided into four classes: (1) analyses of collective-bargaining settlements and wage trends, (2) studies of price behavior in various industries, (3) studies of price behavior cutting across industry lines, and (4) issues in federal regulation. Although there will be no attempt here to describe or catalog all of the studies, individual studies will be presented as

5

examples of different kinds of analyses and of various problems confronting CWPS during its first four years.

Analyses of Collective-Bargaining Settlements. In January 1976 CWPS published a preview of selected major collective-bargaining settlements scheduled to be negotiated during the upcoming calendar year.[5] The purpose of the paper was to provide a general economic background and framework against which individual settlements could be assessed along with a detailed analysis of collective bargaining within the major industries where bargaining agreements were to expire in 1976. Economy-wide trends in wages, prices, productivity, and profits over the preceding decade were presented and compared with corresponding developments occurring from approximately 1973–1976. The recent wage gains of workers in industries covered by the study were placed in a broader perspective and compared with aggregate wage measures and price trends. The analyses of individual collective-bargaining situations included a description of the recent history and structure of bargaining in each industry, an assessment of the size of previous settlements, comparisons of trends in hourly earnings of workers in each industry and broader measures of hourly earnings in the economy as a whole, a discussion of employment trends and selected measures of industry performance, and the outlook for negotiations in 1976.

A similar report was prepared for the 1977 collective-bargaining calendar.[6] This study reviewed 1976 settlements and previewed upcoming negotiations. In addition to these studies, CWPS issued a series of reports on individual collective-bargaining agreements. In these reports, CWPS presented estimates of the total cost of the agreements and assessed the likely impact of the settlements on industry costs, prices, and employment.

Each of these reports contained a breakdown of the total estimated cost of the agreement, including: fixed wage increases; estimated cost-of-living wage adjustments (assuming alternative inflation rates); roll-up, or the additional cost of providing existing benefits, such as vacations and holidays, which increase in cost with increases in the hourly wage rate; employer payments to trust funds for health and welfare and pension benefits; and other fringe benefit improvements. In 1976 the council published reports on settlements in the trucking, rubber, electrical equipment, and automobile industries. Settlements covered in 1977 included steel and communications, and in 1978

[5] CWPS, *1976 Collective Bargaining Negotiations: A Background Paper*, January 1976.
[6] CWPS, *Collective Bargaining: Review of 1976, Outlook for 1977*, February 1977.

CWPS analyzed agreements in the coal and railroad industries.[7]

The council also monitored selected bargaining situations in the construction industry, with particular emphasis on geographic areas such as California and the Pacific Northwest, where the building trades were winning large settlements. On various occasions CWPS met with the parties involved in the negotiations or held a public hearing to manifest its concern about the outcome of these negotiations.

Industry Studies. A variety of factors determined the agenda for the industry studies by CWPS. The downward inflexibility of prices during the 1974–1975 recession made industries such as aluminum candidates for analysis. Other industries such as steel had chronically high rates of cost and price increases and presented the government with demands for trade protection which required an analysis of the relationship between imports and domestic price behavior. Some industries were accused of failing to translate cost moderation into corresponding price moderation, eliciting a CWPS investigation of the pattern of price and cost behavior (for example, for bread and auto parts). In other industries, the relationship between product prices and the ability of the industry to attract new capital and modernize was studied.[8] Finally, CWPS conducted some special studies transcending industry boundaries, including an analysis of the effect of industry concentration on price behavior and a study of the relationships between interest rates and inflation.[9]

It would be difficult to document any impact of these studies on the rate of inflation. Only a fraction of the economy was subjected to scrutiny in this manner, and it is doubtful that those industries that were studied modified their price behavior significantly in response to the CWPS analysis. Yet these CWPS activities were not without value. Like the analyses of collective-bargaining agreements, the industry studies have a potential instructional value and a potential "deterrent" effect. Ironically, however, although the studies focus on private-sector behavior, the likely effect, if any, is on the public reaction to and influence on price determinations. This instructional and deterrent effect typically occurs through a process in which a group such as

---

[7] See CWPS, "An Analysis of the Automobile Settlement," CWPS-225, January 1977; CWPS, "An Analysis of the Master Freight, Electrical Equipment, and Rubber Industry Settlements," CWPS-189, September 1976; and various other CWPS reports.
[8] See, for example, CWPS, "Price Increases and Capacity Expansion in the Paper Industry," December 1976.
[9] See Ralph Beals, "Concentrated Industries, Administered Prices, and Inflation," paper prepared for the Council on Wage and Price Stability, June 1975.

CWPS, by means of an objective analysis of the facts, calls into question the popularly accepted conventional wisdom about price behavior. These studies of price behavior may thwart or forestall misinformed government policies directed to specific industries. A few examples may clarify this point.

The case of steel. The steel industry presents a vivid example of the kind of contribution that a group of analysts can make to public policy decisions. This is not to say that we need a wage-price council, as structured in the late 1970s, to perform this function. Yet an independent group of analysts, outside of the regular government agency network concerned with "industry policy" (that is, outside the office of the special trade representative, outside the departments of Commerce, Labor, and the Treasury), can perform a useful service by providing objective analysis to decision makers. Such analysis can question some of the widely held, often misleading, or incorrect beliefs that can force an administration into costly decisions in a piecemeal, industry-by-industry fashion.

For many years numerous steel industry representatives, public officials, and analysts have clung to the following views about the plight of the domestic steel industry: (1) Japanese and other steel exporters have gained a foothold in U.S. steel markets by capitalizing on periodic domestic labor disputes; (2) these exporters have retained customers "won" during a U.S. strike by an elaborate set of subsidies from their home governments enabling them to "dump" their goods — and, figuratively, their unemployment — onto U.S. shores; (3) in part due to a government-encouraged pipeline of funding for capital improvement projects, the source of the Japanese cost advantage over American steel producers emanated from a superior technology and an edge in productivity; (4) high prices for domestic steel are caused to a large extent by an increased flow of imports, which forces domestic steel mills to produce a lower volume of steel at higher unit costs; (5) if imports could be curtailed to historical levels typical of the 1955–1975 period, the domestic industry's volume would expand significantly, unit costs would fall, and profitability would be restored to respectable levels; and (6) reliance on foreign steel sales — even to the extent of 18 to 20 percent of domestic consumption — is risky, as the Japanese, in particular, will lure U.S. customers with temporary "bargain" prices in a downturn and then extract a painful premium for sales in a boom period or cut off sales altogether. In discussions with industry officials and nonindustry steel analysts over the 1975–1977 period, I discovered how prevalent these viewpoints were and the extent to which they constituted virtually an article of faith for the steel industry and a call to arms for import protection.

8

In the summer of 1977 the drive for import protection gained considerable momentum as a "Steel Caucus" enlisting over 100 members was formed in Congress. Congressional hearings were held, and various members of Congress called for import quotas.

A CWPS report on the steel industry in October 1977, however, produced a very different explanation of the reasons for the industry's plight. The report concluded that the sharp increase in domestic steel prices should be more properly depicted as a *cause* of increased foreign sales to the United States than as an *effect* of rising imports. The Japanese cost advantage over U.S. producers, which was found to be slight after transportation costs were included (particularly in inland markets), was the result of a series of long-term trends rather than short-term intrusions associated with labor disputes. The main longer-term factors contributing to the erosion of the U.S. industry's competitive advantage (the U.S. industry was a net exporter in 1955) were a decline in the cost of raw materials in the world economy compared with the U.S. industry, notable improvements in the efficiency of ocean transport, lower foreign labor costs, and the spread of modern steelmaking technology to other countries.[10]

These same developments enabled countries like Japan to match the United States in labor productivity — even though these countries at first used many more hours of labor to produce a unit of output — and to negate the previous U.S. cost advantages in technology and raw materials. In the late 1970s, according to the report, the source of the competitive edge of Japanese over U.S. firms was their significantly lower rate of labor compensation (Japanese pay rates for steelworkers are about half as high as for their U.S. counterparts) and their ability to construct steelmaking facilities in Japan at costs substantially below those in the United States.[11] The U.S. firms know how to build technologically advanced facilities (in fact, in the post–World War II period, the Japanese learned from the United States how to construct modern steelmaking facilities). The problem facing U.S. firms is that construction delays, the high cost of plant construction, a U.S. environmental policy that is biased against new facilities, and the specter of high operating costs (particularly labor costs) combine to make the construction of new facilities uneconomical.[12] In other words, given the operating cost structure into which U.S. firms have become locked, the

---

10 See CWPS, *Prices and Costs in the United States Steel Industry* [cited hereafter as *Steel Report*], October 1977, pp. 6-12.

11 Ibid., pp. xv, 30-34, 84.

12 For a discussion of this bias in environmental policy, see Robert W. Crandall, writing on the Environmental Protection Agency (EPA), in Crandall et al., "On Saving the Kingdom: Advice to the President-Elect," *Regulation*, vol. 4, no. 6 (November/December 1980), pp. 20-22.

potential reduction in unit costs resulting from the technological improvements associated with the construction of new facilities would not be sufficient to justify the enormous capital outlays needed to complete what amounts to a three-to-five-year project.

It was also concluded in the CWPS report that just as an increase in the overall domestic market share of imports could not be blamed for the poor earnings performance of the U.S. companies, so a retreat of imports from a market share of 18 to 20 percent to levels approximating historical averages for the 1955–1975 period (14 percent) would not improve profitability much. Even if domestic production rose to make up fully for the decline in imports, the favorable effects on domestic output, employment, and unit costs would be quite modest.[13]

Finally, the report called into question the widely held views on the importance of export subsidies to our major trading partners and the notion that the United States would be "cut off" or subject to extortion during subsequent boom periods, leading to a steel shortage or an acceleration of steel price inflation. The study stressed the importance of considering the offsetting effects of exchange-rate fluctuations in estimating the net impact of foreign practices such as border tax rebates, and concluded that the value of various subsidies (for example, value-added-tax [VAT] rebates) offered to foreign steel producers by their governments does not represent a significant share of total production costs. Indeed, there is evidence that, for some of our major trading partners, such subsidies constitute less than 1 percent of total cost.[14] In the CWPS study it was also concluded that the success of the Japanese steel industry could not be attributed to a countercyclical, dual-pricing system of pricing in domestic and world markets. Japanese exports have surged phenomenally over all stages of the Japanese business cycle.[15]

In October 1977, President Carter announced a system of trigger prices for steel mill products, along with several other features, including Economic Development Administration loans for modernization. Although trigger prices represented a protectionist policy, they were less restrictive than a quota on imported steel, which was rejected.

It is difficult to assess what role the CWPS steel analysis played in the decisions made in the administration and Congress in late 1977. Clearly, a variety of economic and political factors affected the outcome of legislative and executive deliberations during this period. At least within the context of decisions made by the president's Steel Task Force, however, which represented a wide spectrum of potentially

[13] CWPS, *Steel Report*, p. xviii.
[14] Ibid., pp. xviii, 91-93.
[15] Ibid., pp. 85-90.

conflicting interests within the administration, this report — and the analysis underpinning it — appeared to be instrumental in stiffening the resistance of the administration to the demands for strong protectionist measures advocated by the congressional "Steel Caucus" and some steel industry representatives.

There is also a sense in which an effort like the CWPS steel study lives to fight again another day, even if its immediate impact is rather limited. The problems of the U.S. steel industry are chronic; temporary booms, as in 1974 and 1979, lessen the political pressure for protection, but the pressure inevitably mounts again when the order backlog for U.S. producers shrinks. The value of an effort like the 1977 CWPS steel industry study may lie in producing an analysis of a problem that competes with the conventional wisdom. The analysis provides ammunition for those government leaders trying to foster free trade. Of course, the policy selected by the Carter administration to deal with rising steel imports — trigger prices — was by no means a free trade stance. The problems involved in this policy will be explained in chapter 4.

One can make the argument, however, that whatever the drawbacks of the ultimate compromise between free trade and protectionist positions (and the package including trigger prices announced in October 1977 was, in my view, such a compromise), it is quite possible that the staff effort which challenged the premises of protectionism contributed to an outcome more consistent with a market-oriented position than would otherwise have occurred. Again, it is difficult to isolate the independent effect of this type of effort in an environment where a multitude of factors are affecting policy. Even though there are instances in which staff analyses gather dust or are disregarded, in my view some of these efforts contribute to sounder public policy.

Other industry studies. Other industry studies completed by CWPS during the 1974–1978 period also challenged popular notions about the underlying causes of price behavior in particular industries. Auto parts prices, for example, rose sharply in 1974–1975, leading to claims that automobile manufacturers compensate for relatively weak performance in some business divisions through excessive price increases for auto parts. Insurance companies protested that price increases for auto crash parts were out of line and were forcing up insurance rates. The findings of the CWPS study were based primarily on a sample of automobile crash and maintenance parts for the four major U.S. automobile manufacturers. Limited information was also gathered from several independent parts manufacturers. CWPS collected its own data sample primarily because of weaknesses in the available measures, including the producer price index for auto parts and the widely publicized but misleading State Farm Insurance Index.[16]

According to the CWPS report, published in May 1977, the sharp price increases for auto parts in 1974 were comparable to the increase in the all-industrial component of the producer price index. Furthermore, auto parts prices were found to have risen much more slowly than consumer or industrial wholesale prices during the period when wage and price controls were in effect, and in line with these broad measures of inflation in 1976. The acceleration in parts prices in the 1974–1975 period reflected rising input prices (particularly steel) and a postcontrols catch-up increase designed to restore profit margins. It was concluded that there was nothing unusual about auto parts prices during this period and that the alarm in some quarters was, in part, based on the upwardly biased insurance industry price index.

In this case, the council's findings, although certainly undramatic, may have helped deflate accusations of excessive price increases primarily by exposing the weaknesses of existing price measures and constructing a more reliable index. Considerable work of this type was also done in industries such as aluminum and automobiles, where the CWPS staff developed and continuously updated its own price index. Typically, this type of effort was undertaken where government or industry indexes either used inaccurate weighting systems for different subgroups of product lines or inadequately reflected transactions prices. In the aluminum industry, for example, the CWPS staff concluded that the Bureau of Labor Statistics (BLS) measure of aluminum prices unduly weighted ingot price changes relative to price trends for fabricated aluminum products. The CWPS index was designed to correct this problem.[17] In the case of steel, the CWPS staff concluded that variations in discounts from list prices were inadequately accounted for in the BLS measure of prices for steel mill products.

In some cases, CWPS, in reports devoted solely to the adequacy of government data, systematically analyzed deficiencies in data series. For example, CWPS sponsored and published a study of the producer price index by Richard Ruggles and prepared a report on data needs regarding employee compensation for state and local government workers.[18]

Other CWPS studies challenged the popular notion that the share of the farm dollar going to so-called middlemen (between farmers and retailers) had increased significantly and questioned the companion

---

[16] CWPS, *Auto Parts Price Behavior: 1971-76*, May 1977.
[17] CWPS, *Aluminum Prices, 1974-75*, September 1976.
[18] CWPS, *State and Local Government Employee Compensation Needs*, October 1976.

view that wholesale and retail farm prices respond faster to increases than to decreases in raw commodity prices.[19] There were CWPS studies that contested the view that industrial concentration per se is an engine of inflation,[20] disputed claims of a shortage of fertilizer, and opposed tax credits for home insulation on the grounds that the demand for insulation was already surging in response to rising fuel bills and supply bottlenecks would inhibit the industry's ability to meet expanded demand, resulting in sharp price increases.

Issues in Federal Regulation

When the Council on Wage and Price Stability was created by Congress, it was given a mandate to "review the activities and programs of the Federal government to discover whether they have any inflationary impact."[21] This mandate was a result of the increasing awareness that in many cases government regulation can raise costs and prices. Much of the activity of CWPS in this area involved performing cost-benefit studies for a wide variety of newly proposed regulations, filing its views with regulatory agencies, and formally opposing proposed regulations whose estimated benefits were not commensurate with estimated costs.

In the 1975–1976 period CWPS reviewed regulations affecting business in areas where expenditures of billions of dollars were at stake; yet it also looked into those areas in which the outlays were relatively small. The latter were seen as establishing an important principle that might have broader applicability. CWPS intervened, for example, in a regulatory dispute involving a requirement to install latches on matchbooks. A large percentage increase in the cost of matchbooks does not add much to consumer outlays, but nonetheless CWPS believed at this time that such regulations should be challenged to foster realistic safety standards at minimum costs.

The types of studies falling into the larger dollar category included an analysis of an OSHA proposal limiting the noise level to which workers could be exposed in an eight-hour day. The CWPS report criticized the OSHA study for not containing an adequate cost-benefit analysis or cost-effectiveness analysis. In attempting to correct this deficiency, the council concluded that the proposed controls would be extremely costly compared with a program which would allow per-

19 CWPS, *The Responsiveness of Wholesale and Retail Food Prices to Changes in the Costs of Food Production and Distribution,* November 1976.
20 See Beals, "Concentrated Industries."
21 James C. Miller III and Bruce Yandle, *Benefit-Cost Analysis of Social Regulation* (Washington, D.C.: American Enterprise Institute, 1979), p. 5.

sonal protective devices, variations in the standard among industries, and a system of penalties based on the degree of hearing impairment. Using a more systematic analysis, CWPS determined that the preceding alternatives could provide the necessary benefits at a much lower cost than the inflexible standard proposed by OSHA.

At this time CWPS also studied a proposal by the Federal Energy Administration which required manufacturers to improve the energy-efficiency of a variety of household appliances. In its analysis, CWPS emphasized that the public should receive the benefits of decreased energy consumption with the least cost (a sacrifice of alternative goods and services).

A further example of the council's cost-benefit studies was an analysis of an EPA proposal to reduce effluent discharges by the iron and steel industry into the nation's waterways. The estimated cost of meeting the standards over a nine-year period, from 1975 to 1983, was approximately $4 billion. Because of the magnitude of these expenditures, the potential adverse effect on prices, the perceived weakness of EPA's inflationary impact analysis, and the belief that the regulations themselves could be modified to be made more cost-effective, CWPS undertook the study of the proposed EPA regulations.[22]

In the 1977–1978 period the council was concerned with transportation rate regulation which put upward pressure on costs and prices and international trade restrictions which eliminated restraints on prices otherwise resulting from import competition. CWPS also continued to support a change in the approach to environmental, health, and safety regulations. The council suggested that penalties, monetary incentives, and flexible performance standards—as opposed to rigid uniform regulations—could significantly reduce costs without a reduction in the intended benefits.

In the latter part of the Carter administration the Regulatory Analysis Review Group (RARG) was created as an independent mechanism for resolving regulatory disputes. CWPS performed a role similar to that of a "prosecutor," appearing before or making submissions to RARG to oppose federal regulations that, according to the council's analysis, did not appear to be cost-effective or to yield benefits in line with costs.

One of the major regulatory disputes brought before RARG involved regulations on cotton dust proposed by OSHA. CWPS argued for the use of personal protective devices and early physical examinations to detect byssinosis, a disease caused by exposure to cotton dust. OSHA pressed for engineering alterations in textile plants that, while far more expensive, were alleged more effective in reducing the disease.

[22] Ibid.

The council supported proposals to lift restrictions on the marketing of reconstituted milk, basing its conclusions on the fact that with such restrictions consumers were unable to purchase a lower-priced alternative to fresh milk and that the current practice increased the price of the product above the price of fresh milk. In addition, when the Department of Labor (DOL) proposed a regulation defining pension plan assets, CWPS responded by expressing concern that there was no analysis by DOL of the regulation's benefits or costs. CWPS also recommended administrative changes in the Davis-Bacon and Service Contract Acts to reduce the upward pressure on wages believed to emanate from the requirement of this legislation that "prevailing wages" be paid by federal contractors.

The council studied the Department of Energy's profit-share bidding system for use in outer continental shelf oil and gas lease sales. CWPS criticized the proposed system for being a large regulatory burden whose benefits may be small and outweighed by the costs of the procedure. CWPS also analyzed federal timber policy and urged a better balance between environmental goals and the availability of an adequate supply of timber to meet the nation's housing construction needs without sharp price increases. CWPS provided various options for increasing the timber yield from national forests without jeopardizing environmental objectives.

Throughout the six years that the council conducted these regulatory analyses, it emphasized the importance of balancing the costs against the anticipated benefits. This was a methodology that was consistent with the mandate of CWPS to identify inflationary activities of the federal government.

3
Wage-Price Guidelines: Auxiliary Policy Tool or Self-Standing Program?

This chapter analyzes the Carter administration's wage-price guidelines in relation to other policies operating during the 1978–1980 period. It focuses on the tension between those guidelines and fiscal and monetary policy initiatives undertaken at the same time. The chapter sketches alternative roles that wage-price guidelines could play in reducing inflation, relative to broader macroeconomic policies designed to remove excessive government stimulus to the economy. This analysis forms the basis for assessing the Carter guidelines.

Alternative Ways of Viewing Wage-Price Guidelines

Proponents of wage-price guidelines argue that the guidelines will attenuate the adverse production and employment effects of government policies designed to reduce the rate of inflation. The wage and price moderation called for by such guidelines, if achieved, is expected to cushion output and employment, to some extent, from the deceleration in the growth of nominal incomes associated with more restrictive government policies.[1] Opponents of guidelines have both questioned their effectiveness as an anti-inflation policy and stressed their deleterious side-effects, including the temptation they provide to government to follow less restrictive fiscal and monetary policies than would otherwise seem advisable.[2]

There are three ways of viewing wage-price guidelines: (1) as an *adjunct* to restrictive fiscal and monetary measures which does not make these measures less vigorous; (2) as having a *parallel*, rather than

[1] See George L. Perry, "Slowing the Wage-Price Spiral: The Macroeconomic View," *Brookings Papers on Economic Activity*, 1978 : 2, p. 288.
[2] See Marvin H. Kosters, testimony before the Joint Economic Committee, Subcommittee on Economic Growth and Stabilization, December 6, 1978, pp. 11-12.

a *subordinate*, role vis-à-vis fiscal and monetary policy; and (3) as having no useful role.

In the first model, the function of guidelines is largely pedagogical—that is, to provide target rates of wage and price increases that point toward, and are consistent with, rates that would be achieved through the successful operation of fiscal and monetary measures. Such targets would act as a signal to labor and business that the government has adopted ongoing measures to remove excessive government stimulus to the economy and, as a result, somewhat lower rates of wage and price gains would be sufficient protection for the private sector against an anticipated lower overall inflation rate. In this conceptual framework, guidelines reinforce and supplement rather than substitute for the required fiscal and monetary restraint. In this context, their job would be to translate a given degree of government restraint into a lesser impact on production and employment rather than to attenuate the degree of restraint needed in the first place. Under this model of guidelines, the targets would not be implemented through a program; there would be no set of rules, regulations, and exceptions, because the targets would provide general guidance, not specific detail to fit every situation.

The second concept of guidelines depicts them as more of a first line of attack against the "momentum" of wage and price increases, which seems to be self-perpetuating. In this conceptual framework, guidelines are expected to reduce, even though they may not fully obviate, the need for government restraint. In the extreme, this viewpoint sees in guidelines per se a prescription for curing rapid rates of inflation and a license to continue fiscal and monetary measures otherwise thought to be overly stimulative, on the grounds that their effects, with the guidelines in place, would be limited to greater growth in "real" variables such as employment.

The choice between an active and a passive role for wage-price standards depends in part upon how one views the wage-price–setting process. Those who view the process as occurring mainly in competitive labor and product markets tend to favor the more passive model, whereas those who view wages and prices as being largely "administered" by unions and companies with market power favor a more active policy. In the passive framework, guidelines are viewed primarily as a means of speeding the process of adjusting wages and prices to market-clearing levels. In the active framework, guidelines are needed to bring wages and prices down from levels above equilibrium and to achieve a lower rate of increase in wages and prices than would otherwise occur. Thus, in the passive model, the intrusion into actual wage- and price-setting processes is very limited, because here the guidelines would establish paths or targets toward which rates of increase should descend. In the active model, however, the intrusion into the wage- and price-setting process is more direct and more immediate, because here the guidelines would establish and enforce specific limits to wage and price increases believed to be determined largely in noncompetitive settings.

In both the active and the passive models, guidelines are seen as a necessary set of signals to private-sector units, based on the notion that expectations about wages and prices will not adjust (or will adjust only after an unacceptable time lag) to changes in government policy. The notion that substantial losses in output would result from a turn to persistent anti-inflationary fiscal and monetary policies (because expectations would not adjust to the new policies) opens the door to a useful role for wage-price targets. Alternatively, such targets would presumably be unnecessary if most wages and prices are judged to be flexible (at least after some reasonably short time lag), if deviations of real output and employment from their "natural" levels are seen to arise from discrepancies between expected and actual wages and prices, and if rational expectations are believed to govern wage and price determination. In effect, this conceptual framework represents a third viewpoint—one that sees no necessary or even useful role for wage-price targets.

George L. Perry views guidelines as an adjunct to fiscal and monetary policies, and believes that this concept should be palatable and useful even to those relying primarily on rational expectations to mitigate the output and employment losses associated with such plans.

> Linking an incomes policy to an announced nonaccommodating policy on aggregate demand would help achieve Fellner's result [reduced inflation]. . .an effective incomes policy would produce a more favorable prospective split between real growth and inflation for any given path of nominal demand growth. Thus, expectations of inflation would change by more than the Phillips curve predicts. And to the extent that expectations do affect current wage decisions — which is still an open question — they would complement an incomes policy. Although it is an incomes policy that changes the immediate trade-off, the nonaccommodating demand policy is a necessary complement. Without it, the reduced inflation promised by the improved trade-off could be dissipated by a movement along the new trade-off curve.[3]

[3] See Perry, "Slowing the Wage-Price Spiral," p. 288. In this article and a subsequent one, Perry articulates his preference for what he calls the "mainline" model over competing monetarist and rational-expectations viewpoints. See George L. Perry, "Inflation in Theory and Practice," *Brookings Papers on Economic Activity*, 1980 : 1, pp. 207-41.

Proponents of the rational-expectations school of thought, however, would not be as quick to accept this reinforcement from guidelines, preferring to rely on the combination of wage-price flexibility and the sensitivity of firms and workers to a credible policy to bring about the required moderation in wage and price trends. In part, this reluctance stems from the fear that the presence of guidelines would adversely affect expectations. According to this view, people would question the likelihood of a persistent anti-inflation posture with guidelines in force.

In fact, the main impediment to moderation in wages and prices from this viewpoint is not so much the market power of firms or unions as it is the prevalence of longer-term contracts in certain sectors of the economy (for example, three-year collective-bargaining agreements in the major union sector of the work force). Rather than adopt guidelines as a supplement to restrictive fiscal and monetary policies, advocates of this position might prefer to develop a mechanism for undoing or revising such contracts if the degree of restraint required was relatively severe.

Whenever wage-price guidelines are established, there is always some prospect for revision of the initial format in which they are presented. Thus what begin as general targets may evolve into rigid limits, and broad rules of thumb may be transformed into elaborate procedures with a rulebook of exceptions. Moreover, guidelines that may be initially proposed in an auxiliary role, with no intention of deflecting fiscal or monetary policies from a steadily anti-inflationary course, once in place may present a temptation to diverge from that course. It is just this kind of vision that causes some observers to oppose any use of wage-price guidelines.

Wage Indexation

The objective of mitigating the adverse effect on employment of slower growth in aggregate demand could also be fostered by a wage indexation plan. Milton Friedman has proposed such plans as accompaniments to less expansionary fiscal and monetary policy. He argues that indexation would reduce the unemployment associated with changes in government policy.[4] Friedman's point is that by automatically lowering wage increases as price increases decelerate, indexing would reduce the loss of production and employment from a more restrictive economic policy. In this role, wage indexation would be comparable to the passive model of guidelines, but Friedman would not favor the use of guidelines.

[4] See Milton Friedman et al., *Indexing and Inflation*, AEI Round Table (Washington, D.C.: American Enterprise Institute, 1974), pp. 2, 18.

An effective numerical wage guideline would truncate the distribution of wage gains, with no downward adjustments (and conceivably some acceleration although there is little evidence of a "floor effect") by those below the standard. By contrast, an economy-wide wage indexation plan would edge all wages down as price increases decelerate and would leave the wage structure intact. Rather than rigidly lopping off the high end of the spectrum of wage increases, an indexation plan would seek a broad pattern of deceleration in a varying array of wage gains. Indexation would freeze the wage structure, however, because it would tend to maintain wage relationships existing at the beginning of the indexation scheme.

More seriously, however, wage indexation is a double-edged sword. Although it can reinforce a policy of slowing the growth in government spending, it can also exacerbate the inflationary effects of an acceleration in such growth. Such adverse effects, of course, are more likely to occur in an economic climate in which resources are almost fully utilized. Kosters has noted that in such a climate the relative responses of prices and output are likely to be asymmetrical.[5] At such a point, further increases in demand could be expected to yield higher inflation with little positive effect on output, whereas a slowdown in demand growth would lead to a less than proportionate reduction in inflation.

Thus, with wage indexation in force, greater importance would be attached to determining government policy. If policy was mistakenly based on the notion that the economy was far from the limits of its productive capacity, then government stimulus would result in greater inflation, as the initial surge in prices was translated more quickly into corresponding wage gains than would occur without wage indexation. The tendency to interpret both the level of the unemployment rate and the rate of capacity utilization as reflecting more slack than actually exists in the economy could heighten the chance that such mistakes would occur. A failure, for example, to account for the fact that higher rates of unemployment today reflect not only the degree of slack in the economy but also the changing mix of the labor force and the effect on the length of unemployment spells of the various income maintenance benefits would cause the government to provide excessive stimulus to the economy. With wage indexation in force, the inflation resulting from this mistake would reverberate more quickly through the economy.

It would be politically difficult to put a wage indexation plan into effect during a time of overall restraint in government macroeconomic

[5] Marvin H. Kosters, testimony before the Committee on the Budget, U.S. Senate, Washington, D.C., March 7, 1979, pp. 4-5.

policies and then remove it when the task of decelerating inflation was judged to be complete. Moreover, with indexation, the government would be inclined to try to prevent all kinds of temporary surges in prices that could otherwise be ignored.

The Carter Guidelines

On October 24, 1978, President Carter announced his wage-price guidelines program. A pay standard limited hourly wage and private fringe benefit increases to a maximum of 7 percent for each employee group in a company. A price standard stipulated that a firm's weighted average prices increase during the ensuing year at a rate at least 0.5 percentage points less than the firm's average price increase during 1976–1977 (but no more than 9.5 percent). The details of these standards—including a variety of exceptions and special rules—are described in chapter 4.

Although the effects of guidelines may be difficult to interpret, President Carter's guidelines were widely viewed as a case of the more active, independent type, despite the administration's presentation of a comprehensive anti-inflation package in 1978 that included a more restrictive fiscal policy and regulatory reform. Against the backdrop of public reaction that the budget, monetary, and regulatory policy pronouncements were largely rhetoric, the guidelines were interpreted as the centerpiece of the Carter policy, and as such, found wanting. This reaction to Carter's standards undermined their effectiveness at the outset. Although accompanied by other policy pronouncements, the 1978 guidelines were seen largely as a *self-standing anti-inflation policy*.

In its white paper on inflation issued in conjunction with the announcement of the standards, CWPS emphasized the need for fiscal restraint. Yet fiscal restraint is treated as a distinct policy tool aimed at what is called one of inflation's several causes, whereas guidelines are justified as a separate anti-inflation policy geared to a different cause of inflation. The white paper argues this way:

> Inflation has several causes. Reducing inflation, therefore,requires that we deal, not just with one, but with several problems:
>
> - Since the economy has come far in its recovery from recession, monetary and fiscal policies must now guard against the emergence of excessive demands and economic overheating that inevitably lead to accelerating inflation.
> - Legislative and regulatory actions to achieve social objectives must be carefully screened to minimize the effects on costs and prices.

- Ways must be found to break the momentum of self-perpetuating price and wage increases that has become so deeply
entrenched in the private sector after ten years of inflation.

A balanced program must address all three of these problems. Trying to attack inflation by concentrating on any one
alone would lead to policies that were either ineffective or
damaging to our economy. In the first instance, relying solely
on highly restrictive monetary and fiscal policies to reduce
inflation, given its strong momentum, would lead to recession. On the other hand, voluntary measures to break the
momentum would not be effective in an exuberant economy,
unrestrained by responsible fiscal and monetary policy.[6]

This exposition suggests that while the administration was mind-
ful of the need for fiscal and monetary restraint in fighting inflation, it
viewed guidelines not so much as reinforcing such efforts as operating
on a villain wholly separate from excessive stimulus — momentum.
The wage-price spiral, according to this notion, seems to have taken
on a life of its own, one that cannot be snuffed out through restrictive
macroeconomic policies, but that requires instead an incomes policy
placing direct limits on wage and price changes. According to this
notion, by itself a policy of steady withdrawal of excessive government
stimulus to the economy is unacceptable because it would not crack
the inflationary spiral without generating a recession. Recession occurs, it is argued, because the momentum of inflation precludes wages
and prices from adjusting to the altered macroeconomic policy stance,
causing a substantial falloff in production and employment. Incomes
policies, in this model, are viewed as a way of slowing inflation without producing such an economic slowdown. Inflation is depicted in
terms of separate components (that is, an overheated economy and
inflation momentum), and there should be a policy to address each of
the components.

In my view, the momentum of inflation is not self-perpetuating,
although it may seem to be so as a result of persistently overstimula-
tive government policies. Perhaps we have become so accustomed to
such policies that they seem inherent in our economic system and
unrelated to their own effects. To attack the momentum of inflation
with guidelines is to attack the symptoms of inflation; the momentum
of inflation is no more a cause of inflation than inertia is a cause of price
stability. Inflation is fed by government policies and will only recede
when those policies are decisively altered.

Although the rhetoric of the Carter economic policy depicted

[6] CWPS, *Fact Book: Wage and Price Standards,* October 31, 1978, p. 2.

restrictive fiscal policy as the handmaiden of guidelines, in reality there was not much restrictiveness. Indeed, while President Carter's FY 1980 and FY 1981 budgets represented some movement to more austerity, at least relative to his two previous budgets, government spending continued to grow sharply. Federal spending in FY 1981 was 34 percent greater than in FY 1979, and off-budget direct loans grew by an estimated 71 percent over the corresponding period ($13.6 billion to $23.2 billion). Indeed, the federal deficits in both FY 1980 and FY 1981 were about $60 billion, although in part this reflects lower than anticipated revenues attributable to the unexpected sluggishness of the economy. Furthermore, monetary policy provided excessive stimulus to the economy as the growth in the monetary aggregates exceeded the targets set by the Federal Reserve. From the fourth quarter of 1978 to the fourth quarter of 1979, for example, the major monetary aggregates increased about one percentage point above the Federal Reserve's target range, and this gap was also one-half to one percentage point over the following year, 1979-IV–1980-IV.[7]

It is claimed that relying solely on fiscal and monetary policies to reduce inflation is unacceptable because it spells an inevitable recession. This notion overlooks two important points: (1) the withdrawal of excessive stimulus need not be abrupt and Draconian though it must be persistent; and (2) the combination of ineffective wage-price guidelines and overly stimulative macroeconomic measures will cause inflation to accelerate continuously, which also will lead to recession. Thus, the choice is not between recession without guidelines, on the one hand, and no recession with them, on the other hand. Rather, the choice is likely to be one of a slowdown in economic activity occurring in the immediate future versus chunks of forgone output that are spread out over subsequent time periods. William Fellner states the choice this way:

> Only in the very early stages of the post-1965 inflationary era was the short-term Phillips trade-off favorable for a few years. By now a trade-off exists probably only in the sense that the output costs of disinflating demand will have to be borne in the immediate future, while the output costs of the continued accommodation of inflationary expectations would be spread out over a period of indefinite length, starting from a lower level but growing rapidly and cumulating.[8]

Moreover, a slowdown in economic activity associated with a with-

[7] M1A actually fell within the range in 1980, but M1B, M2, and M3 growth exceeded their respective targets.
[8] William Fellner, "Comments on Paper by George L. Perry, Inflation in Theory and Practice," *Brookings Papers on Economic Activity*, 1980 : 1, p. 247.

TABLE 1
TRADE-WEIGHTED AVERAGE OF THE EXCHANGE
RATE OF THE U.S. DOLLAR,
OCTOBER 16 – NOVEMBER 3, 1978
(1973 = 100)

October 16, 1978	86.65
17	86.21
18	86.00
19	86.21
20	85.46
23	85.28
24	85.44
25	84.37
26	83.57
27	83.44
30	82.07
31	83.07
November 1, 1978	86.68
2	87.25
3	87.95

SOURCE: Raw exchange rates are from the Federal Reserve Bank of New York, 1978. Weighted averages are computed by the Federal Reserve Board, Financial Markets Section, Division of International Finance.

drawal of excessive stimulus is preferable to the gyrating, erratic course that has characterized macroeconomic policy in recent years, with its inevitable byproducts of both inflation and recession.

This course is characterized by occasional restrictive actions by the authorities which temporarily arrest, but do not reverse, the tendency of inflation to accelerate. These temporary deviations from a basic posture of accommodation tend to be sporadic and unpredictable. They do not stop the ultimate upward trend in inflation because although they may temporarily interrupt the process of rising inflationary expectations, they do not halt it.[9]

We have been on a dangerous roller-coaster ride down precipitous recessions that, at best, temporarily dent inflation, and up government-stimulated recoveries that lead to a reacceleration of inflation. The repeated and capricious sharp turns in economic policy in the 1970s fed inflation and recession.

In my judgment, the wage-price guidelines were initially presented on October 24, 1978, not as an adjunct to a set of fiscal and monetary

[9] Ibid., pp. 243-245.

TABLE 2
EXCHANGE RATES FOR THE U.S. DOLLAR,
OCTOBER 16 – NOVEMBER 3, 1978
(currency units per dollar)

	Deutsche Mark	French Franc	Japanese Yen	SDR[a]
October 16, 1978	1.8700	4.2770	186.20	0.770785
17	1.8408	4.2315	183.80	0.765713
18	1.8300	4.2120	182.30	0.763777
19	1.8463	4.2430	182.75	0.765050
20	1.8227	4.2065	183.50	0.762910
23	1.8027	4.1770	181.10	0.758745
24	1.8172	4.1935	182.20	0.761279
25	1.7820	4.1495	180.20	0.754323
26	1.7626	4.0830	179.50	0.749342
27	1.7610	4.0405	179.80	0.747919
30	1.7285	3.9875	178.50	0.741074
31	1.7367	—	176.00	0.741407
November 1, 1978	1.7735	—	178.50	0.748914
2	1.8635	4.2755	186.00	0.768778
3	1.8890	4.2995	—	0.773103

NOTE: Dashes (—) indicate days when there was no trading because of a holiday.
[a]SDR = special drawing rights.
SOURCE: International Monetary Fund, *International Financial Statistics*, December 1978 and January 1979.

measures, but as an anti-inflation policy in their own right. This policy combination seemed to suggest, at least implicitly, that the risk of recession associated with a policy relying on fiscal and monetary measures alone was unacceptable to the Carter administration. The combined package seemed to be a way of imposing restraint without the normal risk accompanying restraint. World financial markets felt otherwise, however, viewing the guidelines as proof that the administration was not serious about its proposed fiscal, monetary, and regulatory restraint, and interpreted the wage-price standards as *the* administration anti-inflation policy. Finding such a policy inadequate, financial markets registered a vote of no confidence. The adverse reaction in international financial markets put severe pressure on the value of the dollar. Indeed, in the week following the announcement of the guidelines (October 24–31, 1978), the trade-weighted average exchange rate of the U.S. dollar declined 4 percent. (See table 1.) Indeed, in the last two weeks of October 1978 the dollar dropped 6.8 percent against the French franc and 7.6 percent against the deutsche mark. (See table 2.)

On November 1, 1978, against the backdrop of a worldwide clamor for an anti-inflation program aimed more at the cause of inflation than its symptoms and an apparent widespread repudiation of a guidelines strategy, President Carter embarked on an abrupt change in course with his "dollar rescue" program.[10] The combination of a guidelines program and a turn toward more austere fiscal and monetary policies was depicted as an eclectic package designed to cover all bases. In reality, however, the sequence of events in late 1978 reflects not so much the development of a coherent anti-inflation package, of which guidelines were an integral part, as an apparent cave-in of one theory to another. The president seemed to believe the guidelines would be the mainstay of his new anti-inflation policy, but he could not convince the outside world, which demanded that government practice fiscal and monetary restraint.

The outcome of this process can be viewed as a compromise between those who believed that an economic slowdown would arrest the acceleration of inflation and those who believed that guidelines would obviate the need for this harsh medicine. A more likely explanation, however, is that guidelines were expected to be a first line of defense against inflation, and when that line crumbled in an initial assault, a new battle plan was hastily assembled to avert disaster. The wage-price standards appeared to be discredited at the outset, and this impression seemed to be reinforced by White House actions. The brief and tepid defense of the guidelines by the White House, coupled with the apparent concession to the forces calling for austerity, contributed to a feeling that the guidelines were stillborn. There was a sense in which they were damned by the faint praise they received from their own proponents.

The Carter administration's role with respect to the wage and price standards was one of mixed messages. In January 1978, President Carter took the first steps in his anti-inflation program by announcing the following strategy: (1) setting a goal for the deceleration

---

[10] The dollar support package consisted of two parts. First, the United States acquired $30 billion in resources from a joint intervention program with Switzerland, Germany, and Japan. This $30 billion intervention package contained several different items: the Treasury's drawings on the U.S. International Monetary Fund reserve position of $2 billion and $1 billion in deutsche marks and yen, respectively; the Treasury's sales of a total of $2 billion of special drawing rights (SDR) to Germany, Japan, and Switzerland; a doubling of the Federal Reserve swap lines with Germany, Japan, and Switzerland—to $6 billion, $5 billion, and $4 billion, respectively; the Treasury's commitment to issue up to $10 billion in foreign-currency–denominated securities in foreign private markets.

Second, domestic monetary policy was tightened as the Federal Reserve raised the discount rate from 8½ to 9½ percent and imposed a 2 percent supplementary reserve requirement on large time deposits. (For additional information on the dollar rescue program see *Economic Report of the President*, 1979, Washington, D.C., pp. 155-56.

of inflation; (2) becoming involved in major wage and price negotiations; (3) publishing notices of which agreements were out of line with the goal; and (4) demonstrating to the private sector, by the president's actions on government programs, how inflation could be brought under control. Despite the fact that over the next several months the administration failed to follow up on its goal setting and that it participated in several price-raising decisions, including an agreement to protect the steel industry from foreign competition, a settlement of the coal strike with very high wage increases, and a program that would raise prices on several farm products, the public was still expected to exhibit appropriate restraint after Carter announced the specific guidelines in October 1978.[11]

Over the course of the program, there was no forward movement on the fourth element of the presidential leadership strategy. "Little progress was made on the individual microeconomic actions that government could take on its own to reduce inflation"[12] because taken alone the inflationary effects of these individual cases "seemed small and the political costs of conflict with individual interest groups seemed large."[13] In addition, after the initial announcement of the standards, the president and his staff only gave the barest support to the program: there was minimal press coverage of nonconforming price and pay decisions; government contracts were never denied to companies that were violating the standards; and the enforcement powers given to CWPS were ineffective against those companies that were not affected by public opinion.

As a result of the policies of the Carter administration during the period of the 1978–1980 wage and price standards, the "government did not convince the public that it regarded inflation as serious or that it was taking the lead in exercising the restraint necessary to solve the problem."[14] This contributed to the program's demise.

The about-face in anti-inflation policy in October 1978 was characteristic of the ambiguity, uncertainty, and contradictions in economic policy in the 1977–1980 period. Tax rebates were strenuously pursued in early 1977 only to be dropped abruptly in May 1977. The Federal Reserve Board and commercial banks were jawboned in 1977 when interest rates edged upward, yet a subsequent, much sharper run-up in interest rates in early 1980 received the tacit acquiescence of the

[11] Robert W. Hartman, "The Budget and the Economy," in Joseph A. Pechman, ed., *Setting National Priorities: The 1979 Budget* (Washington, D.C.: The Brookings Institution, 1978), pp. 56-57.
[12] Barry P. Bosworth, "Economic Policy," in Joseph A. Pechman, ed., *Setting National Priorities: Agenda for the 1980s* (Washington, D.C.: The Brookings Institution, 1980), p. 63.
[13] Ibid.
[14] Ibid.

White House. Instead of jawboning this rise in interest rates, the White House imposed credit controls in March 1980; they were removed later in 1980, and in October 1980 interest rate hikes were again publicly criticized by the administration. The FY 1981 budget proposed in January 1980 was substantially revised in March 1980 and modified again throughout the year.

Such zigzags in anti-inflation policy generate uncertainty among the public. Impulsive policy changes lead to fickle, unpredictable public expectations, which in turn can be roadblocks to real economic growth.

Confusion over the Causes of Inflation

The repeated, abrupt changes in administration policy also reflected a fundamental confusion about the causes of inflation. The sequence of economic policy steps in the fall of 1978 lacked a coherent framework to hold together the various pieces of the anti-inflation strategy. On the one hand, the guidelines program announced on October 24, 1978, implied that direct intervention in wage and price decisions could reduce the need for the more indirect and seemingly more painful route of reducing wage and price increases by creating some slack in labor and product markets. Moreover, the program seemed to blame inflation on business and labor. On the other hand, a week later the dollar rescue program seemed to be an overnight conversion to "the old-time religion," signifying that the administration felt that eorts to circumvent an economic slowdown would be imprudent and self-defeating. The guidelines package directed responsibility for inflation away from Washington, whereas the dollar rescue package returned that responsibility to Washington. Thus the lack of cohesion between the two different steps made it seem as though the wage-price guidelines contradicted, rather than supported, the primary thrust of the administration's anti-inflation policy.

An Alternative Conceptual Framework

The notion that there is a self-perpetuating cycle of wages and prices that must be broken with an incomes policy shows the confusion over the causes of inflation. The cause of a steady acceleration in overall inflation must be distinguished from various factors that contribute to a temporary increase in the general price level or to higher price levels in individual sectors of the economy.

In my view, an appropriate conceptual framework views developments such as oil price shocks or a sizable Teamster wage agreement not as causes of a continuous acceleration in inflation per se, but as developments that initially alter relative wages or prices and generate a temporary acceleration of inflation. Of course, increased prices for a particular good raise costs for those who buy it, which in turn may lead to an increase in the demand for alternative goods and higher prices for substitutes. Similarly, higher wages for Teamsters, for example, raise transportation costs in many industries and may lead ultimately to some substitution of nonunion workers and owner-operators for Teamsters. Whether such shocks or realignments translate into an acceleration in overall inflation, however, depends primarily upon how we react to them. It is important to distinguish between the forces initiating some shock to the domestic economy and the force perpetuating generalized inflation.

Sometimes a price shock such as the 1979 oil price increases by the Organization of Petroleum Exporting Countries (OPEC) affects the costs of so many firms and households that it appears to be a cause of generalized inflation. Although price shocks do have widespread effects in the economy, they are not necessarily associated with an acceleration of the overall inflation rate. These price shocks force policy makers to make a difficult choice. If a price shock is not accommodated, the price will eventually be beaten down, but the cost of this strategy can be considerable. In Switzerland, for example, a refusal to accommodate the oil price shock in the 1973–1975 period was accompanied by a drop in national output of about 10 percent.

If a price shock is accommodated, however, a precipitous decline in output can be postponed, if not avoided, but the cost of this strategy is likely to be an acceleration in inflation. It is the postponement of the pain (or, in Fellner's terms, taking the output loss in a series of smaller chunks) that may explain the attractiveness of the accommodation strategy. Most politicians prefer delayed costs to immediate costs. Over time, however, the ability to delay costs with continual accommodation will tend to evaporate, and this effect both narrows and clarifies policy choices.

As argued earlier, we may have become so inured to the effects of accommodative demand-management policies that we overlook the critical part they play in the inflation acceleration process. Rather than acknowledging that such policies enable and facilitate the continuous acceleration in inflation, there is a tendency to look for someone to blame. In this sense, OPEC is a handy villain, one that can be (and has been) used to excuse and divert attention from the more fundamental cause of ongoing inflation. Thus, we have witnessed the government blaming an acceleration in inflation on OPEC, on a drought that leads to a run-up in raw farm commodity prices, or on the Teamsters. All of these become ready and quite visible targets of government scorn, while the basic process by which inflation rolls on is obscured.

Let us consider a case in which a sharp increase in crude-oil prices is not accommodated by an acceleration in the growth of the money supply. What forces impede a corresponding increase in the broad measures of wages and prices? The restraint of demand for goods and services can perform this limiting role. The demand for labor services, for example, may be constrained because a run-up in import prices generates no corresponding increase in domestic employers' revenues. Rising oil prices therefore provide no additional profits from which to pay for an acceleration in domestic wage increases. Indeed, the rising cost of imported fuel will squeeze domestic profits and may also adversely affect labor productivity. Thus, if employers' ability to pay larger wage increases is restricted by a combination of sluggish profits and flat labor productivity, wage increases on an economy-wide basis may not accelerate despite a temporary acceleration in inflation attributable to soaring fuel prices.

Indeed, it is futile to accelerate the growth of the money supply in an attempt to "cheat" the diminution in real incomes associated with accelerating price increases that provide no concomitant ability to pay correspondingly higher wages. The resulting acceleration in generalized inflation will erode the purchasing power of the higher pay. Selected groups of workers whose particular labor contracts provide considerable insulation from the wage implications of these economy-wide problems will at least temporarily increase their wage premium relative to the average worker, but this realignment in relative wages need not be associated with, nor would it necessarily bring about, an acceleration in average wage gains.

Moreover, oil price increases do not automatically translate into price increases for all goods and services, even those that are significant users of oil. The domestic prices of steel or automobiles, for example, do not rise automatically with increased energy costs, at least over short periods of time when profits may absorb a portion of rising costs. Firms in these oligopolistic industries are still constrained by their respective demand curves, and price increases will be limited by consumers' options of buying comparable products from foreign producers.

A similar cautionary note must be sounded regarding attempts to depict specific wage increases as inflationary. In addition to raising costs directly, an increase in compensation rates for Teamsters or auto workers may indeed affect the wages of other workers (for example, butchers who work with Teamsters in supermarkets or farm implement workers who follow the pattern of the auto settlement), thereby indirectly raising costs across a broad spectrum of the economy. There may also be wage imitation effects (as when steelworkers try to match gains obtained by autoworkers). Such recognizable wage patterns, however, do not translate into an economy-wide framework for wage determination. The existence of selected wage-to-wage influences is not inconsistent with the notion that overall average wage changes will be largely affected by labor market conditions and inflationary expectations. In other words, one does not have to deny the importance of relative wage comparisons in various isolated circumstances (for example, for plumbers and electricians in the same city) in order to believe that such considerations are not the primary driving force behind trends in overall average wages.[15]

Moreover, recent research suggests that significant relative wage effects involve union workers adjusting to wage changes of nonunion workers, rather than vice versa.[16] This suggests that the problem of wage stabilization is not one of limiting major union settlements to pull down the average wage rate (for which guidelines might seem appropriate), but rather one of finding the appropriate macroeconomic policies that would foster a deceleration in overall wage increases, which would subsequently decelerate union wage changes.

[15] See Daniel J. B. Mitchell, testimony before the House Budget Committee Task Force on Inflation, June 26, 1979.

[16] See Marvin H. Kosters, "Wage Standards and the Interdependence of Wages in the Labor Market," in William Fellner, *Contemporary Economic Problems, 1979* (Washington, D.C.: American Enterprise Institute, 1979), pp. 233-60. See also Robert J. Flanagan, "Wage Interdependence in Unionized Labor Markets," *Brookings Papers on Economic Activity*, 1976 : 3, pp. 635-73.

4
Wage-Price Guidelines:
A Case of Regulatory Expansion

There was a sharp conflict between the Carter administration's commitment to reduce or simplify government regulations and its launching in October 1978 of potentially the most complex of all regulatory programs — a detailed program of wage-price guidelines. In each major anti-inflation statement during the 1977–1980 period President Carter pledged to reduce the burden of federal regulation. Yet, ironically, wage-price guidelines were juxtaposed with separate regulatory initiatives or commitments whose purposes they seemed to frustrate and whose intentions they seemed to belie.

The conflict between wage-price guidelines and the goal of regulatory reform was inevitable because the guidelines were issued as a program designed to provide standards of behavior tailored to a wide variety of special circumstances. In this respect, the Carter guidelines differed from the Kennedy-Johnson guideposts, which were relatively straightforward and undifferentiated numerical standards that were not accompanied by handbooks, fact sheets, and question-and-answer pamphlets.

In terms of format, the Carter standards were quite similar to Phases II–IV of the Nixon controls, as both featured a detailed set of rules. In this respect, the Nixon controls gave people experience with a set of rules, procedures, and exceptions that provided guidance for later rule makers. This is not to argue that there were no important differences in the precise rules adopted, but rather that the apparatus and basic structure of the two programs were quite similar. In this sense, there has been a kind of evolution of wage-price policy, beginning with discussions of wage-price standards in the economic reports of the president in the second Eisenhower administration and the informal general numerical standards of the Kennedy administration. The latter were toughened up under President Johnson (until they were discredited and abandoned in 1966), but the policy remained one of generalized standards. The Nixon controls were modeled more closely on the Korean War wage-price controls than on any of the precursors of the 1960s. And the Carter guidelines continued the Nixon model, albeit in an allegedly voluntary framework.

With its guidelines, the Carter administration ventured into the area of regulation and lost its footing. The advertised simplicity of the program, thought by some to be the rationale for distinguishing it from controls, vanished quickly. The result was a labyrinth of specific new regulations which seemed to undercut the administration's commitment to deregulation in a few specific industries.

Some Arbitrary Distinctions in the Application of Wage-Price Guidelines

It is important to distinguish between the technical and political aspects of establishing a wage-price policy. In a technical sense, the task can be viewed as an effort to replicate the decisions of the market in most circumstances and improve on the outcomes a market would have generated in instances where the government believes that market outcomes need improvement. In this sense, the task involves ascertaining which markets feature a range of discretion in wage or price determination, isolating those markets, and trying to move the wage or price setters down toward the lower end of the range. Competitive markets are either to be left alone, or the authorities will try to replicate the market outcome. In this exercise the key empirical questions are: (1) Where are the cases where a band of discretion exists? and (2) How large is this band? An examination of these issues under a mandatory-controls experience suggests that such situations are hard to find and, where they exist, the range of discretion seems small in terms of the magnitude of the inflation problem.[1]

In a political sense, the task of the wage-price authorities can be depicted as that of giving the appearance of bearing down on strong economic units while actually imposing the standards on relatively weak economic units. Ironically, those players in the economic system who are most likely to be targeted for controls on the substantive grounds that they have market power are also the ones whose political power is equal to the task of deflecting government intervention away from their decision making. Thus, government parries with big companies or big unions, scolding them for "outsized" price or wage increases and periodically setting up confrontations (in which

[1] See Marvin H. Kosters, with J. Dawson Ahalt, *Controls and Inflation: The Economic Stabilization Program in Retrospect* (Washington, D.C.: American Enterprise Institute, 1975).

government often loses) with these units. These confrontations are really phony wars; the real battle is between government authorities and the weaker economic units. Any impact of the standards is likely to result from their direct effect on the weaker groups, which in turn may ultimately have an indirect effect on the stronger groups. A wage standard may be "tested," for instance, by collective-bargaining agreements of the Teamsters or the autoworkers, but if such a standard has any effect at all, it is likely to work through an initial dampening of wages in the nonunion sector. This deceleration in nonunion wages could be followed by a deceleration in union wages as relative wages are restored to previous levels.[2]

Proponents of guidelines argue that by moderating or postponing increases in a measure of inflation such as the consumer price index, guidelines will set in motion a chain of events (for example, a smaller settlement for the Teamsters) that will crack inflationary momentum. This improvement, if it can be achieved, can only be bought at the cost of a certain amount of inefficiency in the economy. Advocates of guidelines would hope to minimize inefficiency by limiting guidelines to noncompetitive industries.

Inherent in the notion of wage-price guidelines is a concept that individual wage or price setters have a range of discretion regarding the establishment of wages and prices. The very concept of guidelines implies that wage and price standards should be applied to wage and price setters — that is, to those wage earners and firms with a sufficient degree of market power to affect the price of these services or products. In other words, to the extent that firms and workers are believed to be playing some type of active role in sustaining an acceleration of inflation, standards must be brought to bear on those actors and players in the system that have a significant degree of discretion over prices and wages. Accordingly, designers of wage-price guidelines or controls typically attempt to limit their effective coverage to those having a discretionary range for maneuver, while trying to avoid applying them to purely competitive markets where they would be more likely to cause a misallocation of resources.[3]

Although designers of wage-price programs might wish to aim their remedies specifically and solely at industries and labor markets having a substantial concentration of power, technical limitations arise

[2] Marvin H. Kosters, "Wage Standards and the Interdependence of Wages in the Labor Market," in William Fellner, *Contemporary Economic Problems, 1979* (Washington, D.C.: American Enterprise Institute, 1979), pp. 233-60.

[3] Of course, such misallocations are not the exclusive province of competitive industries. See Frank Camm, Charles E. Phelps, and Peter J. E. Stan, "Resource Allocation under the CWPS Price Guideline: The Case of Fixed Proportions," Rand Corporation Report R-2634-DOE/RC, May 1981.

from both the difficulty of delineating competitive and noncompetitive markets and the problem of making the line stick once it is drawn. In other words, there are two tricky questions: (1) When is a market purely competitive, or how broad a band of discretion over price determination is required to determine that an industry should be covered? and (2) How does one convince those whose degree of discretion slightly exceeds the yardstick that the line cannot be adjusted a little to accommodate (exempt) them?

The price standard announced in October 1978 excluded sales by producers of goods and services in the following categories from the calculation of a company's average price change: (1) agricultural, fishing, forestry, and mineral products; (2) recyclable scrap materials; (3) commodities whose historical and current price changes are closely tied to price movements on an organized open exchange market, either domestic or foreign; (4) exports; (5) deliveries during the program year; (6) products exchanged in other than open and arm's-length transactions; (7) new or discontinued products; (8) custom or one-time product sales; (9) interest rates.[4]

This conventional list of categories to be excluded from guidelines includes not only those ignored because they are believed to have no influence over price determinations (that is, price takers), but also those dropped for administrative convenience (for example, custom products or new products). Also, aside from such markets as corn, soybeans, scrap, etc., there are surely industries in which firms have only a narrow band of discretion over prices, despite their departure from a textbook model of pure competition. Although wage-price programs arbitrarily divide the economy into competitive and noncompetitive sectors, using lists of standard categories for exclusion, in reality there is a spectrum of varying degrees of competition, including variations not only in a firm's influence over price but also in such factors as barriers to market entry.

The attempts to delineate competitive industries that do not need guidelines inevitably injects new arbitrariness into a wage-price program. As indicated, commodities whose prices are tied to an open exchange or auction market were exempt from the price standard. In 1979, however, CWPS decided that copper prices were exempt while lead and zinc prices were not. Copper producers, however, had only recently linked their prices to the Commodities and Exchange Market (COMEX), and domestic copper price changes — particularly price declines — have frequently lagged behind movements in the world price of copper. By contrast, lead prices have been tied to an exchange

---

[4] CWPS, *Pay and Price Standards: A Compendium*, June 1979, p. 2-1.

for years, but the lead industry did not receive an exemption.[5]

Similarly, raw farm products were exempt from the price standard, but if any processing took place, product prices were expected to conform to the standard. The line delineating raw from processed foods, however, becomes blurred (pork bellies, for example, were judged to be processed, although they are traded in an open exchange market).

These same blurred distinctions could be found in the application of the pay standard. Following the initial issuance of the pay standard, the CWPS staff was flooded with notices of proposed pay adjustments from companies or unions asking CWPS to agree that one of the several exceptions to the standard applied to their cases. There were exemptions or exceptions for low-wage workers (below $4 per hour), deferred wage increases under prior collective-bargaining agreements, tandem relationships between two groups of workers, labor shortage situations, and gross inequities or hardships.[6] The first two criteria were relatively clear-cut, but the latter three were subject to varying interpretations or to dispute. The council's definition of a tandem pay relationship,[7] for example, excluded many situations that some felt should have been encompassed by this exception. Inevitably, the lines dividing the exempt from the nonexempt were arbitrary. Labor negotiations cannot be neatly divided into those with and those without a leader-follower relationship, with nothing in between. Whether a particular labor market is facing a shortage depends in part on the scope of the market area, the time frame considered, and the flexibility of the relevant wage to rise and clear the market.

The Growing Complexity of Applying Wage-Price Guidelines

Even voluntary standards initially seen as providing only general guidance to business and labor (as the Carter standards were initially described) inexorably evolve into a complex set of rules and regulations. Once the decision is made to have a rule book and to determine how the standards apply to individual cases, that rulebook will expand continuously, and the initial "simplicity" of the program unravels. A growing body of exceptions, exclusions, and exemptions emerges as the standards are applied to individual cases.

---

[5] Ultimately, the lead industry received an exemption, but in early 1979 its efforts for equal treatment with the copper industry were thwarted by CWPS.

[6] CWPS, *Pay and Price Standards*, pp. 2-4.

[7] The definition of a tandem pay increase required the establishment of a clear pattern of a leader-follower relationship along with pay increases that were equal in value and directly related in timing.

When the government decides whether to honor a company's or a union's request for an exception, it frequently sets a precedent — that is, it makes policy, if only inadvertently. Often these decisions involve trading program effectiveness for increased fairness. The guidelines are "tried on" by individual firms. In some cases they do not fit, so the government, in an effort to be fair, tailors the general standard to fit the particular situation. The customer goes away happy. Others, witnessing this, come in for their alterations.

In complying with the price standard, companies had to determine what constituted a company, a custom product, a new product, and so on, and each of these determinations involved ambiguity or blurred distinctions. A custom product, for example, was defined as one with "substantial design changes." What constitutes "substantial"? Companies were told that they should decide this themselves, but they were also told that to bid on government contracts they must certify themselves to be in compliance with the standards. Unsurprisingly, companies demanded more guidance. Equally unsurprising, new regulations and new exceptions were spawned. Each new ruling, each new exception, set a precedent that others understandably tried to exploit, leading to difficulties no matter where and when the line was finally drawn.

Consider the kinds of equity problems that arise from decisions giving special treatment to particular industries or groups of workers. Shortly after the guidelines had been issued, special standards were developed for firms in the retail food and retail trade industries, essentially allowing them to dispense with price monitoring and use instead a mark-up or profit-margin criterion. Because retail firms typically sell thousands of products, establishing a base period rate of price increase would be a heroic — if not an impossible — task. Yet other industries that face data retrieval and organization tasks nearly as formidable as those of the retailers were nonetheless forced to comply with the price standard. A price standard for the real estate industry, for example, makes no more sense than one for retail trade. Yet there were no special rules for such groups, who were left on their own to determine how to fashion a monitoring and compliance plan. Although all industries of this sort pose special problems for a program designed essentially for industries like steel, tires, or automobiles, some were issued special standards and others were not.

Furthermore, even within the sectors covered by the regular price standard during the 1978–1980 period, there was an arbitrary distinction drawn between those with uncontrollable cost increases and others whose costs were presumably controllable. The latter were allowed to dispense with the price standard — that is, they did not have to decelerate the rate of increase in their weighted average prices — and convert to a profit-margin criterion. Other industries were complying with alternative gross margin standards. By CWPS estimates, only about one-third of the firms falling within the purview of the standards were actually under the basic price limitation.[8]

In addressing the problem of wages, the administration initially singled out major union workers as the culprits and pointed out that many large unions had won pay gains of 9 to 10 percent per year in the 1976–1978 period, widening the gap between their pay and that of the average worker.[9] If big unions were the source of concern, though, why insist that every employee unit in the country hold its compensation gains to 7 percent per year?

Moreover, if major union wage increases were viewed as a chief cause of inflation, it is puzzling to observe that compliance with the pay standard was made so much easier for union workers than for nonunion workers. From the exemption of deferred increases under contracts negotiated prior to the program, to treating cost-of-living escalator clauses as if inflation were 6 percent (it was actually 12 percent during the first year of the program), to allowing an 8 percent first-year increase for union workers in multiyear agreements, the government's pay standard favored union workers. These features of the standards program might be defended on the ground that there is a need to recognize the realities of collective bargaining if there is to be any chance of moderating labor settlements. My point here is to note the contradiction — the public pronouncements scolded unions, the actual standards favored them.

Adding to the equity problem between union and nonunion workers were changes in the standards announced in December 1978. The changes excluded major elements of the cost of employee benefits, specifically: (1) any portion of the increased cost of maintaining previously negotiated health benefits that exceeded 7 percent per year, and (2) employer pension contribution increases required by changes in actuarial assumptions or funding methods rather than by improvements in benefits. The revised guidelines in this instance treated workers with light benefit packages more harshly than those with heavy benefit packages and rewarded those workers whose pension plans had not been fully funded or properly administered. Thus, on the one hand, the guidelines were not well adapted for the worker who took most of his compensation package in the form of wages and paid a

---

[8] See CWPS, *Evaluation of the Pay and Price Standards Program,* January 16, 1981, p. 28.
[9] See Barry P. Bosworth, address to the Associated Press Annual Meeting, Atlanta, Georgia, May 1, 1978, p. 14. Barry P. Bosworth, testimony before the Joint Economic Committee, July 20, 1978, p. 9.

significant portion of his health care premiums himself (or provided for his retirement primarily through social security and personal savings rather than an employer retirement plan). On the other hand, the guidelines were customized for the worker who traded some portion of potential wage increases for additional health or pension benefits.

Obtaining Compliance through Compromise

Alterations in pay and price standards are designed to make compliance seem reasonable to workers and firms and to reduce inefficiency. Almost every alteration to make the standards more palatable or efficient, however, also weakens and complicates them, and the compromises frequently involve dangerous trade-offs. The application of the guidelines to the trucking industry in 1979 presents a good example.

When CWPS excluded from chargeable pay the actuarially mandated pension contribution increases, it permitted the Teamsters, in effect, to go well over the pay standard and still be in compliance. The Teamsters also received concessions from the government that involved disregarding twenty-one cents of the first-year wage payment and the final cost-of-living escalator payment, which would have been about twenty-three cents at 6 percent inflation. Using the same inflation assumptions, I estimated the cost of the agreement at 29 percent over three years compared with the 22½ percent gain (or exactly a 7 percent per year annual rate) derived by the administration.

The bargaining process seemed to be one in which the union searched for as many loopholes in the guidelines as possible, while the government tried to strike a balance in which enough concessions were granted to obtain the appearance of Teamster compliance (thereby avoiding a showdown or a major setback to the program), but not so many concessions as to vitiate the anticipated influence of the program on day-to-day wage adjustments affecting workers with less political strength than the Teamsters. In this case the union was negotiating with the federal government while employers were third-party observers.

Besides suggesting a fundamental lack of sincerity, there are two difficulties with this tactic. First, with compromises like these the government sends the wrong signals to the private sector and unintentionally fosters inflation. Exempting part of the cost of maintaining previously negotiated health benefits or actuarially mandated pension contributions from a pay cap encourages people to think (incorrectly) of these costs as something apart from the inflation problem. Similarly, "pass-throughs" granted for minimum-wage increases (through the low-wage exemption to the pay standard) and the increase in the cost of compliance with federal regulations suggest (falsely) that these cost items are uncontrollable.

Second, there is a temptation for the government to gain compliance with its standards by giving way on other initiatives that are more vital to long-term economic efficiency. The administration's position on the 1979 labor negotiations in the trucking industry illustrates this point. When initial Teamster wage demands exceeded the guidelines, the administration threatened the Teamsters (and management) with regulatory reform. It could be inferred from this that compliance by the Teamsters would produce the opposite result — that is, deregulation of the industry might have been postponed or shelved.[10]

In addition to loopholes, the president's proposed program also had sweeteners (the proposed real-wage insurance program) and sanctions (barring noncomplying firms from government contracts). The real-wage insurance program would have run the risk of a substantial increase in the federal deficit to entice workers to comply with the pay standard. This proposal was not given serious consideration by the Congress.[11]

The legality of barring noncomplying firms from government contracts was challenged in litigation brought by the American Federation of Labor–Congress of Industrial Organizations (AFL-CIO). After an initial defeat in the federal district court, the government's debarment of noncomplying firms from winning federal contracts was held to be within the president's authority in a June 22, 1979, ruling by an appeals court.[12] Despite the legal victory, however, the government never used this sanction during the life of this program.

Even if sanctions had been used, they would have done little to make the guidelines more effective. They would have further jeopardized support in the private sector for the wage-price program and set bad precedents for federal regulatory policy. Using the right to bid on government contracts as a "club in the closet" would select for special harsh treatment those limited segments of the business community that depend on government contracts for survival, while virtually bypassing most other businesses, and it might even spur inflation by denying contracts to the lowest bidder because that bidder is not in compliance with the standards. Finally, with the Davis-Bacon and Service Contract Acts supporting wages from below and guidelines limiting wages from above, the government in effect would become the wage setter for firms doing any business with it.

[10] Although the trucking deregulation bill passed Congress easily in 1980, the prospects for passage in early 1979 were quite uncertain.
[11] For more information about this proposal, see *Real Wage Insurance*, Legislative Analysis (Washington, D.C.: American Enterprise Institute, 1979).
[12] See CWPS, *Pay and Price Standards*, p. 4.

Other weapons or sanctions that the administration threatened to use to gain compliance included relaxation of import restrictions and reductions in floors set under various wages and prices.[13] These types of procompetitive policy changes, however, should not be made contingent upon firms' apparent noncompliance with wage-price standards. If these weapons or sanctions are not punishments but remedies, they should not be predicated on proving wrongdoing. If they are in fact legitimate punishments, then there is still the danger that they may miscarry, being set in motion by levers chosen for their availability rather than for their appropriateness. They may not hurt the guilty, or they may hurt the guilty and the innocent as well. So, the government must try to set a policy that uses remedies and punishments appropriately.

The Immense Task of Wage-Price Regulation

Wage-price guidelines share with other regulatory programs that displace the market the problem of finding a workable substitute for market decision making. Whenever this "displacement" of the market is attempted, equity must be granted; the government, being visible, cannot be the "invisible hand" that guides us to the efficient solution. The displacement of the market entails the collection, organization, and interpretation of enormous amounts of information. What makes the guidelines program unusual compared with other regulatory initiatives is the sheer immensity of this task as a result of the need to obtain this information, make decisions, and carry them out for virtually all markets.

The enormity of the task becomes more apparent if we imagine replicating in other markets an effort made by the CWPS staff in late 1977 and early 1978 to construct a system of trigger prices covering each steel mill product. The trigger price mechanism was designed to expedite and simplify investigations of dumping by foreign steel producers and was intended as a substitute for formal lengthy antidumping investigations by the government. The calculation of the system of trigger prices was undertaken by five people on the CWPS staff, and it required about five months. The result was only rough approximations of the cost differentials needed to construct a network of trigger prices. The CWPS staff, who were by no means experts on steel, tried to ascertain how much of a cost differential to attribute to the difference between 17-inch and 18-inch diameter steel pipe, how much to allow for zinc coating of sheet, for various chemical treatments to add strength, for the difference between hot finished bars and cold finished bars, and so on. The staff, which had

[13] See CWPS, *Fact Book: Wage and Price Standards*, October 31, 1978, pp. 13-14.

41

never worked in the steel industry (although it had attempted to study the industry carefully), made judgments about the effective yield of finished steel emanating from a given input of raw steel, about the total compensation of steelworkers including complex calculations of the cost of fringe benefits, and about the impact on average unit costs of sharp variations in the volume of sales.

Moreover, these judgments had to be made not only for U.S. steel producers (the CWPS staff was at least familiar with some but by no means all of the institutional characteristics of the domestic steel marketplace), but also primarily for Japanese steel producers, whose costs for each type of steel product became the basis of the trigger prices. Japanese firms operate in a very different environment and typically employ a different mix of technology to produce a ton of steel. Japanese firms, for example, are generally more highly leveraged than their U.S. counterparts, make greater use of contract labor (complicating the calculation of average total labor costs), make greater use of continuous casting, which improves the effective yield, and sell steel to trading companies (in some cases located in the United States), which in turn sell it to users at prices that may reflect international trade strategies and cross-subsidies among various products handled by these trading companies.

Each of the decisions the CWPS staff made would help some U.S. steel companies and hurt others, depending on such factors as their respective product mixes and technology (for example, blast furnaces versus electric arc). Representatives of the steel companies presented data showing that the CWPS differential was slightly off the mark according to their own experience. Other industry representatives complained that CWPS had unfairly separated steel mill products from fabricated products and that their products should not be called "fabricated" (so that those products could then slip in under the protective umbrella of trigger prices). Indeed, it was made abundantly clear to CWPS that the trigger price that was one person's boon (keeping down costs for steel producers) was another's bane (propping up steel prices, which are costs to steel buyers).

It would certainly be a tremendous undertaking to construct a system of "allowable" prices for all markets. The government again faces a difficult choice. It can devote five man-months to gathering data on each market (and still not have all the necessary information), in the process amassing a large staff, spending large sums of money, and forcing private firms to spend much larger sums to make ongoing compliance calculations.[14] Alternatively, it can make judgments based

---

[14] Of course, these outlays by firms are only a portion of the total cost of a measure such as the trigger price mechanism, which, if it has any clout, will also lead to losses for consumers.

on insufficient information in an effort to keep things manageable—or more politically acceptable in the short run with results more economically unacceptable in the long run.

In this sense, wage-price guidelines present a larger-than-life picture of the problems facing all regulators. The differences are not so much in kind, as (enormously) in degree. Ultimately, they reflect an assessment that it is politically necessary to do something and politically inexpedient to do what is economically necessary.

The Need for a Broader Perspective on Regulatory Effectiveness

There has been a tendency to evaluate the impact of a wage-price program solely in terms of whether the intended benefits — a deceleration of inflation — have actually occurred. In the next chapter, the evidence on this question will be critically evaluated. It is worth highlighting here, however, the need for a broader perspective on the effectiveness of regulation. Such a view would weigh the savings from a regulatory program, if any, against the costs — administrative costs, compliance costs, reduced access to goods or services, and quality deterioration — attributable to that program. A more balanced approach that asks at what price any demonstrable cost reductions were purchased yields a more complete picture of program effectiveness. It is difficult to quantify the costs of a wage-price program (and also, as is shown in Chapter 5, difficult to calculate the benefits), but it is important to be aware that they exist.

It is worth noting in this regard that many regulatory interventions have been predicated on a notion of market failure. The underlying presumption is that a market failure has led to such a vast degree of overspending in that market that regulatory mandates to reduce spending will necessarily improve consumer welfare. This concept needs to be qualified in two ways: (1) the observation that consumers are spending more on certain goods or services than they otherwise would if the basic market ingredients of an effective price mechanism, the absence of entry barriers, and good information were fully operative does not mean that any spending cutbacks will make consumers better off or that government planners should decide the optimal amount of spending; and (2) the concept of market failure must be balanced by the corresponding notion of regulatory failure.[15] Markets often depart in practice from their textbook design, but the same is true of regulation. Wage and price regulators, like all regulators, can be overwhelmed by constantly changing circumstances, by technical

[15] See Charles Wolf, "A Theory of Non-market Failures," *Public Interest*, vol. 55 (1979), pp. 114-33. Also, see S. Breyer, "Analyzing Regulatory Failure: Mismatches, Less Restrictive Alternatives, and Reform," *Harvard Law Review*, vol.92 (1979), pp. 549-609.

difficulties in taking over the market role, and by the difficulty of devising an effective implementation design. There can be considerable slippage between the hypothetically achievable regulatory objectives and the actual results. Yet the regulatory solutions are politically appealing because the complexities of the marketplace are often more apparent than the complexities of regulatory procedures. This misperception generates a demand for regulation, but efforts to fill this demand become embroiled in and frustrated by such factors as the inability of regulatory bodies to define their output and the difficulty of separating regulatory inputs and outputs.[16]

Regulatory Experience in Various Sectors of the Economy. There are lessons for wage-price policy from government regulatory experience in individual sectors of the economy. Clark Havighurst has argued, for example, that there is no reason to believe that regulation to keep health costs from escalating will not run into the same problems that plague regulation of surface transportation, communications, and other fields. These problems include the tendency of the regulated interests to gain the ear of the regulators and deflect regulatory policies that appear harmful to them, the impossibility of controlling all the inputs and outputs of regulated firms (which is a particular problem in health care, where outputs are so hard to define), the inefficiencies emerging from the cost-plus character of rate controls, the inclination to shelter the regulated interests from outside competition, and the encouragement of excessive investment of resources in the regulated activity.[17]

In a comprehensive report to the Carter administration on health care, Alain Enthoven stressed the dangers of relying on regulation to solve the problem of rising health costs.

> In recent years, the main line of Government policy has been to attack the problems created by inappropriate incentives with various forms of regulation, e.g., planning controls on hospital capacity, controls on hospital prices and spending, controls on hospital utilization, and controls on physician fees. The weight of evidence, based on experience in many other industries, as well as in health care, supports the view that such regulation is likely to raise costs and retard beneficial innovation.[18]

Skepticism about regulatory solutions also emerges from the

[16] Wolf, "Non-market Failures."
[17] Clark C. Havighurst, "Federal Regulation of the Health Care Delivery System," *University of Toledo Law Review*, vol. 6, no. 3 (Spring 1975), pp. 581-87.
[18] Alain C. Enthoven, "Consumer Choice Health Plan: An Approach to National Health Insurance Based on Regulated Competition in the Private Sector," unpublished report to Joseph A. Califano, secretary of the Department of Health, Education, and Welfare, September 22, 1977, p. 5.

growing body of evidence from other sectors of the economy that have relied heavily on regulation. Many of these industries are now moving away from regulation.

The airline industry provides an example. Regulation of the airlines by the Civil Aeronautics Board (CAB) was defended on the grounds that it held down costs and assured service to remote areas. Careful studies indicate, however, that unregulated airline fares in intrastate markets were less than half the fares of CAB-regulated interstate routes of comparable length and density.[19] The effect of airline deregulation has been to lower fare increases without jeopardizing (indeed enhancing) service to smaller communities.[20] In fact, smaller communities are probably better served now than when the CAB forced the major carriers to serve them and subsidize that service by overcharging travelers going between major cities. Commuter airlines have sprung up or grown to meet the demand, and now have a greater opportunity to compete vigorously with larger carriers.

This situation is analogous to the one in health care, where the current labyrinth of regulation thwarts innovative plans, props up the traditional (and usually larger) health insurers, and leads to inefficient cross-subsidization. Similarly, pipeline tariffs are higher in regulated interstate markets than in unregulated intrastate markets.[21]

Today the country is moving away from regulatory approaches in both the oil and natural gas industries, where regulation is increasingly being viewed as a part of the problem rather than the basis of a solution. Although there is evidence that regulation has lowered natural gas prices, this is primarily because pipeline companies that buy gas at the wellhead are themselves regulated. As Roger Noll has argued, below-market natural gas prices are not a blessing but a problem for consumers, because they create shortages of a fuel that does not create serious environmental damage, reduce new customers' access to natural gas, and threaten existing customers with the disappearance of their principal home fuel supply.[22]

[19] See David R. Graham and Daniel P. Kaplan, "Developments in the Deregulated Airline Industry," Staff Paper, Office of Economic Analysis, Civil Aeronautics Board, June 1981. For an analysis of the cost of trucking regulation see James C. Miller III, "The Costs of Trucking Regulation to Consumers," Transportation Consumer Action Project Symposium on Trucking Regulation and Consumer Prices, Washington, D.C., May 17, 1979.

[20] See, for example, C. C. Barnakov, Jr., "International Air Fare Levels: An Evaluation after Three Decades of IATA Rate-Making," Washington, D.C., U.S. Department of Transportation, 1978, p. 36.

[21] Paul W. MacAvoy, "The Regulation-Induced Shortage of Natural Gas," *Journal of Law and Economics*, vol. 14 (1971), pp. 190-97; see also Andrew S. Carron and Paul W. MacAvoy, *The Decline of Service in the Regulated Industries* (Washington, D.C.: American Enterprise Institute, 1981).

[22] Roger Noll, "The Consequences of Public Utility Regulation of Hospitals," Institute of Medicine, *Controls on Health Care* (Washington, D.C.: Institute of Medicine, National Academy of Sciences, 1975).

5
Assessing the Effectiveness
of the Wage-Price Standards

One means of assessing the degree of adherence to pay and price guidelines is to compare the prices of goods produced with various measures of wages. This is a more appropriate approach than comparing consumer prices with wages. The latter comparison can be misleading because a price standard invariably affects only a subset of prices, and price regulation typically centers on the wholesale prices of goods produced. Moreover, the full impact of the consumer price index (CPI) was not an accurate measure of average living costs during the guidelines period because some items that were included in the measure, such as new homes, are purchased very infrequently. Furthermore, higher prices for items such as imported oil or mortgages do not generate the higher business income that would in turn facilitate the payment of higher wages.

The distinction between using the CPI and a variable such as the implicit price deflator for the nonfarm business sector is germane to the issue of whether wages of workers have fallen behind inflation and to assessments of the effectiveness of the standards. Pay increases did not keep pace with consumer prices during the two-year period corresponding to the guidelines program. (See table 3.) It is tempting to conclude from this development that the wage standard was successful in stopping a price explosion from feeding through to wage acceleration. There are other reasons, however, for the disparity of wage and price trends during this program. First, wage adjustments are typically less subject to significant short-term variation than are price adjustments. Second, significant variations in productivity, related to both cyclical and secular trends, can translate a steady pace of wage increases into a more uneven pattern of price increases. Moreover, energy prices and mortgage interest rates increased sharply through much of the program period, and both raw material prices and interest rates were excluded from the CWPS program.

When measures of employee compensation are compared with the prices of goods produced in the nonfarm business sector, the gap

TABLE 3
Economic Indicators of Wage and Price Changes under the Carter Guidelines
(percent)

Index	Year Prior to Program (1977-III –1978-III)	First Program Year (1978-III –1979-III)	Second Program Year (1979-III –1980-III)
Hourly earnings index	8.4	8.2	9.0
Total hourly compensation	8.6	8.9	9.8
Labor productivity	0.3	−1.7	−0.4
Unit labor costs	8.2	11.1	10.3
Implicit price deflator	6.6	9.0	10.0
Consumer price index	8.3	12.1	12.7
Real hourly earnings index	0.1	−3.6	−3.2

NOTE: The hourly earnings index (current and constant dollars) and consumer price index are measured from September to September (the wage-price program began on October 24, 1978). Other series are measured from third quarter to third quarter. The hourly earnings index covers the private nonfarm sector of the economy, whereas the other measures (except the CPI) cover the nonfarm business sector of the economy.

SOURCE: U.S. Department of Labor, Bureau of Labor Statistics, "Industry Analytical Ratios," special tabulation, February 27, 1980; *Economic Report of the President*, Washington, D.C., January 1980, pp. 244, 259; and U.S. Department of Commerce, Bureau of Economic Analysis, unpublished data.

between wage and price increases disappears. For instance, the implicit price deflator for the nonfarm business sector rose by 9.0 percent over the first program year (third quarter of 1978 to third quarter of 1979), virtually the same pace as the corresponding 8.9 percent gain in total hourly compensation. In the second program year, the corresponding figures were 10.0 percent and 9.8 percent (see table 3).

Furthermore, the rough balance between pay and price increases, as measured by these indexes, occurred despite the drop in both productivity and profits during this period. In the first program year the 11.1 percent increase in unit labor costs in the nonfarm business sector was two percentage points greater than the deflator for the output of this sector. Indeed, in both 1978 and 1979 the deflator increased substantially less than unit labor costs, whereas in 1980 the two indicators, which typically run in tandem over longer time periods, approached a rough balance again (see table 3).

Cast in this light, the data on employee compensation, productivity, profits, and prices are difficult to reconcile with the notion that the pay standard was a binding factor largely responsible for wage restraint. It seems more likely that the failure of wages to accelerate sharply in the face of double-digit increases in consumer prices was due to poor productivity and the sluggishness of corporate profits, which made it difficult for employers to afford larger wage increases.

Assessing the Independent Effect of the Standards

It is important to distinguish the independent effect of the wage-price standards from the impact on inflation of a variety of other factors. Observed average wage trends may roughly correspond to a pay standard for reasons largely unrelated to that standard. Wage increases, for example, may decelerate as a response to weakened aggregate demand. This may reflect a lagged response to a policy of slower growth in the monetary aggregates and more stringent fiscal policies initiated in tandem with a set of wage-price guidelines. Also the standard may be set at a level near expected outcomes to avoid policy contradictions that discredit the program. Such overlapping complicates the task of isolating the independent effect of the guidelines. Similarly, it is easy to conclude that a wage standard is more effective than an accompanying price standard when price increases temporarily exceed wage increases, even though the erosion in real earnings may come largely from factors unrelated to the standards.

Thus, it is important to distinguish measures of what has actually happened with the standards in place from notions about what might have happened in their absence. Also, evaluating the effectiveness of the standards is different from assessing the degree of correspondence between them and observed wage and price trends. In making either assessment, however, one must confront problems such as the weaknesses of government measures of employee compensation, which frequently exclude important components of pay, and the confusion surrounding which elements of labor costs to include under the rules of a wage-price program.

Ascertaining the independent effect of a guidelines program on wage and price trends requires the use of econometric techniques. Two basic approaches have been used in such studies. The simulation approach estimates wage and price equations for some time period ending just prior to the implementation of the wage-price standards. Then, patterns of wages and prices are simulated for the period covering the standards program under a hypothetical no-standards assumption. This procedure simulates what would have happened to wages and prices had there been no standards, based on past trends. Finally, the hypothetical trends during the program period are compared with actual trends to ascertain the effect of the standards. An alternative method of assessing program impact involves estimating wage and price equations through a period including the standards program, with a dummy variable (equal to one during the period) to represent the effect of the program.

Before evaluating the evidence such techniques have produced regarding the effectiveness of the Carter program, it is useful to explain some of the inherent limitations of these approaches. Regarding the simulation approach, to the extent that wage and price equations inadequately explain the behavior of wages and prices prior to the program, they will provide a poor basis for simulating wage-price behavior after the program is started.[1] Second, some observers argue that wage-price standards work not so much by formal program decisions as through altering the nature of wage and price decision making in various sectors of the economy. Yet, the simulation approach is predicated on the notion that the equation based on pre-program experience would have fit well throughout the program period (and beyond) had the program never existed.[2] Thus, the structural equations estimated through the prestandards period could be a misleading guide for simulating the effect of the standards. In other words, if wage-price standards alter the rules of the game, it would be dangerous to estimate their impact based on the old rules.

Similarly, during both the last year of the Nixon controls (mid-1973 to mid-1974) and the period corresponding to the Carter guidelines, an extraordinary leap in the prices of fuel and other raw materials occurred, and it is questionable whether the precontrols equations are still useful in estimating the hypothetical no-controls scenario in view of the complex impact of such relative price changes on the economy.[3]

A final problem concerns the assumption that the amount of stimulus given to the economy by the fiscal and monetary authorities is exogenous to the controls program. According to this assumption, if controls have any slowing effect on inflation, the authorities would provide less stimulus to nominal income than before the program, with real variables such as production and employment remaining unchanged. This assumption seems questionable in view of the temp-

---

[1] Of course, even if the equations "explain" history well, this may still be the case. The sums of squares were minimized for the period of estimation itself; so there would normally be a poorer "fit" for the projection period.

[2] Alan S. Blinder, *Economic Policy and the Great Stagflation* (New York: Academic Press, 1979), p. 117.

[3] Such equations may contain a variable such as energy prices designed to control for other extraordinary events occurring during the period. This would assume, however, that only energy prices and the controls were "different" during the program period.

tation that a wage-price program provides to increase the government stimulus to the economy.

As for the dummy-variable approach, it is difficult to capture all the factors that were different during the controls period through the use of a dummy variable. This approach assumes, somewhat heroically, that the deviations from longer-term wage and price trends observed during the program period are solely attributable to the impact of the program.[4] Also, the validity of this approach hinges on the presumption that all of the coefficients of the model other than the constant term remain the same in the precontrols and program periods, a drawback similar to the one mentioned earlier in connection with the simulation approach. This method has been criticized by Lipsey and Parkin and by Oi.[5] Finally, the dummy-variable specification used in most studies implies that wage-price standards shift only the intercept and not the slope of the wage or price equation. Furthermore, the use of a single dummy variable for the presence of wage-price standards assumes that the standards were either "on" or "off," whereas in fact most standards programs evolve through various phases corresponding to different degrees of monitoring intensity and a varying scope of coverage. Among the many econometric analyses of the effectiveness of the Nixon program, only the study by Alan S. Blinder attempts to distinguish among such phases. Blinder estimates the fraction of the consumer price index under controls in each month.[6]

Blinder has also highlighted the importance of accounting for the phenomenon of postprogram catch-up effects. This problem affects all econometric evaluations of wage-price programs irrespective of whether simulation techniques are involved. Blinder notes that apparently favorable effects of wage-price standards while they are in place can be negated by catch-up increases that may begin as the standards are gradually relaxed and accelerate when they are entirely removed. In fact, his findings indicate that nontrivial favorable effects on the order of 1 to 1.5 percentage point reductions in wages and prices can be more than offset by catch-up.

[4] Blinder, *Economic Policy*, p. 117.
[5] See Richard G. Lipsey and J. Michael Parkin, "Incomes Policy: A Re-appraisal," *Economica*, vol. 37 (1970), pp. 1-31; and Walter Y. Oi, "On Measuring the Impact of Wage-Price Controls: A Critical Appraisal," in K. Brunner and A. Meltzer, eds., *The Economics of Price and Wage Controls*, Carnegie-Rochester Conference Series, vol. 2 (Amsterdam: North-Holland, 1976).
[6] Blinder, *Economic Policy*, p. 125. Although Blinder's adjustment for program intensity is superior to the assumption of a monolithic program, it is still a crude correction. The toughness of the policy—in its articulation and enforcement—may be more important than the proportion of price decisions directly affected. A factor such as toughness would be quite difficult to quantify.

TABLE 4
BLINDER'S ESTIMATES OF THE EFFECTS OF CONTROLS ON THE
CONSUMER PRICE INDEX, 1971–1977

	Percentage Effect on the Price Level						
Month	1971	1972	1973	1974	1975	1976	1977
January	—	−0.66	−1.17	−1.62	+0.84	+0.92	+1.00
February	—	−0.76	−1.15	−1.66	+0.90	+0.92	+1.01
March	—	−0.87	−1.14	−1.59	+0.93	+0.93	+1.02
April	—	−0.96	−1.14	−1.34	+0.93	+0.93	+1.04
May	—	−1.02	−1.16	−0.95	+0.93	+0.94	+1.04
June	—	−1.07	−1.23	−0.60	+0.92	+0.95	—
July	—	−1.12	−1.36	−0.28	+0.92	+0.95	—
August	−0.10	−1.16	−1.44	0	+0.91	+0.96	—
September	−0.16	−1.18	−1.46	+0.24	+0.91	+0.97	—
October	−0.31	−1.20	−1.49	+0.44	+0.91	+0.98	—
November	−0.38	−1.21	−1.53	+0.61	+0.91	+0.99	—
December	−0.46	−1.22	−1.57	+0.75	+0.91	+1.00	—

NOTE: Underlines indicate timing of phases as follows: Phase I, August–November 1971; Phase II, November 1971-December 1972; Phase III, January 1973-May 1973; Freeze II, June 1973-August 1973; Phase IV, August 1973-April 1974. Dashes (—) indicate months when controls were not in effect.
SOURCE: Blinder, *Economic Policy*, p. 128.

Blinder's study of the Nixon controls found that when Phase II ended in late 1972, the price level was an estimated 1.2 percentage points lower than it would have been in the absence of controls, and that no further progress was achieved in the Phase III period. Following the appearance of more favorable effects in the summer of 1973 "Freeze II," the controls reached their maximum estimated effect of 1.66 percentage points in February 1974, whereupon, according to Blinder's estimate, the catch-up began to overwhelm the direct effects of the controls.[7] The price level is estimated to have returned to the level it would have achieved without controls in August 1974—only four months after the controls were removed entirely. From this point, prices began to rise faster than they otherwise would have increased, ultimately leaving the price level about 1 percent higher as a result of controls. Thus, during the twelve months beginning February 1974, when a 1.66 percentage point reduction in prices was indicated, and ending February 1975 when a 1 percentage point increase in prices was

[7] Ibid., p. 128.

recorded, the controls program is judged responsible for 2.6 percentage points of additional inflation.

This outcome, of course, is not really surprising, because the only way in which the price level would be lower after an interlude of controls is if such controls led to improved real performance of the economy (given the assumption that other variables such as monetary and fiscal policy are exogenous). Table 4 reflects Blinder's monthly tracking of the impact of controls on the price level and highlights the importance of accounting for postprogram effects in an econometric assessment of program effectiveness.

Professor Oi also emphasizes the need to include both precontrols and postcontrols time periods in any analysis of the effectiveness of controls:

A maintained implicit assumption of these models is that there are stable pseudo-equilibrium paths of wage and price adjustments to disequilibrating shocks described by the time paths of the unpredictable (but presumably exogenous) explanatory variables. There are compelling reasons to expect that workers and firms will not follow the same pseudo-equilibrium adjustment paths (which prevailed in the absence of controls) in the period just preceding and following the imposition of binding wage-price controls. Their responses in anticipation of or in reaction to controls will manifest themselves in structural changes in the wage and price equations in the periods adjacent to the controls experience. In the light of these considerations, the discrepancies between actual and predicted rates of wage/price inflation must be estimated via the simulation approach for a comparison period extending before and after the period of controls in order to get an estimate of the full impact of controls in retarding the rates of wage and price inflation.[8]

Additional support for the notion that the postcontrols period must be accounted for comes from a thorough study of the effectiveness of incomes policies in Europe by Lloyd Ulman and Robert Flanagan. These authors document numerous cases of postcontrols catch-up effects that eclipse or overpower apparent favorable effects while the programs were in force.[9]

These results have great significance for an evaluation of the Carter pay and price standards. The Blinder, Oi, and Ulman-Flanagan

[8] Oi, "On Measuring the Impact of Wage-Price Controls," p. 45.
[9] Lloyd Ulman and Robert Flanagan, *Wage Restraint: A Study of Incomes Policies in Western Europe* (Berkeley and Los Angeles: University of California Press, 1971).

admonitions can help us to place preliminary verdicts offered by others in a better perspective. With this in mind, we can now turn to how the Council on Wage and Price Stability evaluated its own program effectiveness.

Interpreting the CWPS Estimates

The Council on Wage and Price Stability has estimated both the direct effects of the pay and price standards and their full effect (allowing for the interaction between wage and price increases) for the period from the fourth quarter of 1978 through the third quarter of 1980.[10] CWPS explored both the simulation approach and the dummy-variable approaches (called the direct-estimation method), and their results can be summarized in table 5.

This table indicates that CWPS finds about a 1 percentage point reduction in wage inflation attributable to the standards over the approximately two-year period under study. The effect was found to be somewhat stronger during the period roughly corresponding to the first year of the program (1979) than during the second year (for example, 1.3 percentage points versus 0.8 percentage points, respectively, using the direct-estimation approach for direct effects only). The CWPS analysis finds no significant effect of the standards on prices (except as may occur indirectly through wages). Thus, the following discussion will focus on the CWPS findings concerning the impact of the standards on pay rates.

The first observation about these results is that they show pay standard effects about the same size as or smaller than the initial estimate of the impact of the Nixon controls program on wages. The full CWPS regression results using both the simulation and direct-estimation techniques found essentially no effect of the Nixon controls on wages in Phases I and II of the Economic Stabilization Program (ESP-I)[11] and a 1.1 percentage point reduction in wages during the ESP-II period (Phases III and IV). The corresponding estimate of the impact of the Kennedy-Johnson guideposts on wages was −0.86 in both equations.[12]

These results are consistent with earlier findings by W. Kip Viscusi, who found a pay standard impact on employee compensation of −1.2 percentage points and −1.0 percentage points over the period

---

[10] See U.S. Council on Wage and Price Stability, *Evaluation of the Pay and Price Standards Program,* Washington, D.C., January 1981, pp. 98-99.
[11] The coefficient was actually positive (0.3) in both regressions, but was not statistically significant.
[12] See CWPS, *Evaluation of the Pay and Price Standards Program,* p. 98.

TABLE 5

ESTIMATED IMPACT OF THE PAY AND PRICE
STANDARDS ON WAGE AND PRICE INFLATION,
1978-IV – 1980-III
(average effect over the period, in percent)

	Direct Effect		Full Effect
	Simulation	Direct estimation	Simulation
Wage inflation	−1.0	−1.0	−1.2
Price inflation	−0.8	−0.3[a]	−1.5

NOTE: Pay is measured here by multiplying the BLS average hourly earnings index by the ratio of total compensation to the value of wages and salaries, both from the National Income Accounts. Prices are measured by the consumer price index.
[a]Not statistically significant.
SOURCE: CWPS, *Evaluation of the Pay and Price Standards Program*, pp. 98-101.

TABLE 6

SUMMARY OF ESTIMATED EFFECTS
OF CWPS STANDARDS ON WAGE AND PRICE INFLATION

	Wage Inflation		Price Inflation	
	CWPS	Viscusi	CWPS	Viscusi
Carter guidelines	−1.2	(−1.0)–(−1.2)	(−0.3)–(−0.8)	−0.5
Nixon controls				
ESP-I	0.3	(0.5)–(0.6)	−1.2	−1.4
ESP-II	−1.1	(−1.7)–(2.1)	2.2	(−0.3)–(−0.5)
Kennedy-Johnson guideposts	−0.9	a	0.5	a

[a]Not estimated.
SOURCES: CWPS, *Evaluation of the Pay and Price Standards Program*, pp. 98–101; and Viscusi, "The Impact of the Carter Pay/Price Standards," p.10.

through 1980-II, using ordinary least squares and two-stage least squares regression techniques, respectively.[13] Viscusi also found positive, insignificant signs for the ESP-I variable, and a slightly larger negative effect of ESP-II (2.1 percentage points and 1.7 percentage points).

13 W. Kip Viscusi, "The Impact of the Carter Pay/Price Standards," paper presented at the American Public Policy Management Conference, Boston, Mass., October 1980, p. 10.

54

The comparison of all these findings in table 6 will help put the CWPS preliminary results regarding the effectiveness of the pay standard into perspective.

Viewed in this context, the CWPS findings suggest that even if its results are accepted as reliable preliminary indications of the impact of the standards, the standards are unlikely to have been responsible for any lasting impact. None of the CWPS preliminary estimates of the impact of the Carter standards on wages or prices, for example, is as large as Blinder's estimated impact of the Nixon standards, if one uses the figure of 1.6 percentage points taken near the end of the Nixon program. Yet Blinder's results show that even these larger apparent program effects washed out a year later. Indeed, the seemingly sizable program impact, viewed prematurely as the Nixon program was phasing down, actually yielded ultimately to a perverse effect as the price level was found to be a little higher than it otherwise would have been in the absence of controls. The Blinder results are also consistent with the work of Robert J. Gordon, who found that apparently favorable effects during the Nixon controls period were totally dissipated during the postcontrols period.

In a preliminary assessment of Phases I and II, Gordon finds that wages and prices under controls increased at annual percentage rates of 0.68 and 1.85, lower, respectively, than would have occurred without controls. He concludes, however, that "it is hard to see that any 'success' has been achieved by the temporary control program, since a passing reduction in inflation hardly seems worth the effort that businessmen, lawyers, and government officials have invested in the program.[14]

In a later article, Gordon reinforced his skepticism:

The aggregate equation for nonfood products net of energy, when extrapolated after the end of its sample period in mid-1971, confirms my earlier conclusion that the U.S. price controls held down the price level by a maximum of 3.5 to 5.1 percent, depending on the initial date chosen for the sample period. All of the control effect was reversed during 1974-75, and the price level is now within one-half percentage point of the level predicted in the absence of controls.[15]

Viewed in this light, Viscusi's finding of a negative effect of the Carter

[14] Robert J. Gordon, "Wage-Price Controls and the Shifting Phillips Curve," in *Brookings Papers on Economic Activity*, 1972 : 2, p. 418. For a more sanguine view of the preliminary effect of controls, see Barry P. Bosworth, "Phase II: The U.S. Experiment with an Incomes Policy," *Brookings Papers on Economic Activity*, 1972 : 2, pp. 343-83.
[15] See Robert J. Gordon, "The Impact of Aggregate Demand on Prices," in *Brookings Papers on Economic Activity*, 1975 : 3, p. 655.

pay standard on pay (1.01–1.2 percentage points) that is smaller than his estimate of the impact of the Nixon standards during ESP-II (1.7–2.1 percentage points) does not make one very confident about a lasting impact from this program. The preliminary CWPS program effects are also no larger than, and in some cases not as large as, corresponding temporary effects associated with various incomes policy experiments in Europe, which generally gave way to poststandards catch-up phenomena.[16]

Finally, as stated earlier, it is important to note that the econometric evidence focuses on the existence of the benefits of controls — that is, whether inflation decelerated. As Gordon observes, however, it is important to compare these benefits with the costs of these programs. Such costs are difficult to quantify, because they primarily involve distortions in resource allocation or shortages of goods.

Studies by Marvin H. Kosters and the Organization for Economic Cooperation and Development (OECD) completed after the Nixon controls period stressed the importance of weighing the problems associated with controls against any temporary deceleration in wages and prices. Kosters found little evidence of industries where controls led to a deceleration of prices (except for health care) and found that controls led to shortages, distortions, or plant closures in industries producing meat, fertilizer, concrete reinforcing bars, mining roof bolts, bailing wire, and selected petrochemicals.[17]

GAO's Sensitivity Analysis

Until this point, this study has accepted the CWPS evaluation of its wage and price standards at face value; only the interpretation of those results has been questioned. The findings on program effectiveness, however, are highly sensitive to the exact specification of the equations. An examination of this sensitivity factor further undermines the confidence that can be placed in the preliminary CWPS findings of program effectiveness. A 1980 General Accounting Office (GAO) report on the Carter standards emphasized the importance of accounting for the sensitivity of econometric results to slight variations in the

---

16 See Ulman and Flanagan, *Wage Restraint,* and Anne R. Braun, "Three Decades of Incomes Policy: Reflections on the Role of Incomes Policies in Industrial Countries, 1945-74," International Monetary Fund, Research Document, Washington, D.C., September 1974.

17 See Marvin H. Kosters, *Controls and Inflation: The Economic Stabilization Program in Retrospect* (Washington, D.C.: American Enterprise Institute, 1975), pp. 92-98; and Organization for Economic Cooperation and Development, Working Party No. 4 of the Economic Policy Committee, "The Recent United States Experience with Wage and Price Controls," Paris, May 1975.

specifications of the equations reflecting legitimate alternative assumptions.

Thus, even if these methods show strong evidence for the effectiveness of the standards, that evidence cannot be viewed as absolutely conclusive because the possibility would remain that something other than the standards caused wages or prices to diverge from their historic pattern of behavior. This shortcoming is also present in our own modeling. One implication of this shortcoming is that any claim for the effectiveness of the standards should be supported by more than a single specification of the relevant relationship — that is, by more than one specific formulation of a wage equation such as equation (1), in which all of the choices mentioned above have been made. If the evidence of effectiveness is contingent on a specific model, then less confidence can be placed in the evidence than if effectiveness is demonstrated under a wide variety of reasonable specifications.[18]

GAO used a preliminary CWPS estimate of a -1.58 percentage point effect of the standards on pay rates[19] and varied several of the assumptions underlying the initial CWPS pay equation. The GAO results (table 7) showed that the size of the estimated standards effect fluctuated greatly and was sensitive to the exact method of measuring several of the key variables.

Particularly noteworthy in the GAO sensitivity analysis is the effect of switching from one measure of price inflation to another. The substitution of the personal consumption expenditures deflator (PCE) for the CPI causes the standards coefficient to be cut nearly in half (from -1.58 to -0.92), whereas the further substitution of the nonfarm business deflator for the personal consumption deflator reduces the estimated effect of the standards on pay by another two-thirds (from -0.92 to -0.31) and causes the standards variable to lose its statistical significance.

Following the GAO report in December 1980, CWPS published a final report in January 1981 that included its own sensitivity analysis. The CWPS final results show that two variations in its initial specification of the pay equation caused a sizable range to open around its final estimate of a 1 percentage point reduction in pay inflation attributable

---

[18] General Accounting Office, *The Voluntary Pay and Price Standards Have Had No Discernible Effect on Inflation*, PAD-81-02, December 10, 1980, p. 52.
[19] This estimate was prepared prior to the final CWPS evaluation cited earlier and was a little larger than the estimate of the effect of the standard emerging from the council's preferred equation in this final report.

TABLE 7
Various Estimates of the
Effect of the Pay Standards

	Percentage Reduction in the Average Annual Rate of Wage Increase 1978-IV – 1980-I
CWPS estimate	−1.58
GAO variations	
Seasonally adjusted	
wage index	−1.43
Alternative measures of inflation	
Personal consumption deflator	−0.92
Gross domestic product of	
nonfarm business deflator	−0.31[a]
Alternative unemployment measurement: change in U replaces	
change in $(1/U)^b$	−1.07[a]
Nonfarm business deflator replaces CPI and change in U replaces	
change in $(1/U)$	−0.17[a]

[a]Statistically insignificant at the 5 percent level (one-tailed test).
[b]U represents the unemployment rate.
SOURCE: General Accounting Office, *The Voluntary Pay and Price Standards*, p. 57.

to the standards. The substitution of the percentage difference between potential and actual gross national product (GNP) for the unemployment rate for civilian workers (adjusted by a measure of the natural, or full-employment, unemployment rate) as a measure of labor market disequilibrium has a rather dramatic effect on the pay standard variable, raising its coefficient from −1.0 to −1.7.[20] Similarly, the substitution of the Fixed Weight Personal Consumption Expenditures Index for the CPI as the basic price variable in the wage equation lowers the estimated pay standard coefficient from −1.0 to −0.5.[21] The latter figure is not statistically significant at the 5 percent confidence level. The effect of the CWPS sensitivity analysis on the coefficient of the standards variable is summarized in table 8.

Although it is possible to make an argument in favor of either the CPI or the alternative inflation measures, as well as to justify a variety of different measures of the impact of labor market conditions on

[20] See CWPS, *Evaluation of the Pay and Price Standards Program*, p. 100.
[21] Ibid., p. 102.

TABLE 8
RESULTS OF CWPS PAY EQUATION SENSITIVITY ANALYSIS:
COEFFICIENTS AND T-RATIOS OF THE
WAGE-PRICE STANDARDS VARIABLE[a]

	Coefficient	t-ratio
1. Basic pay equation	−0.978	−2.020
2. Longer lag on CPI	−0.933	−1.921
3. Use of GNP gap instead of unemployment rate	−1.664	−3.625
4. Use of unemployment rate for prime-age males	−0.845	−1.759
5. Dropping the change in minimum-wage variable	−1.156	−2.264
6. Use of alternative variable for Nixon controls	−0.896	−2.289
7. Shorter sample period	−0.834	−1.566
8. Shorter sample period plus use of PCE instead of CPI	−0.514	−1.034
9. Shorter sample period and use of ratio of home purchase costs to PCE as price variable	−0.319	−0.658

[a] For the complete pay equations, see table source.
SOURCE: CWPS, *Evaluation of the Pay and Price Standards Program*, p. 101.

wages, the point here is that a justifiable set of assumptions different from those used by CWPS causes the alleged short-term effects of the pay standard to fade quickly into statistical insignificance. GAO interpreted the results of the sensitivity analysis as undercutting the CWPS claim of program effectiveness:

> Our results show that econometric evidence for the Council's claim that the pay standard restrained wage increases is shaky. Minor variations in the specification of the equation used by the Council to estimate the effect of the standard cause dramatic changes in that estimate. All of the equations we examined fit the data as well as the equation the Council analyzes, but the equations uniformly show a smaller effect of the standard than the Council claims. In several, the estimated effect is essentially zero. Similar results were obtained when we used a simulation to estimate the effect of the pay standard.[22]

[22] General Accounting Office, *The Voluntary Pay and Price Standards*, p. 57.

CWPS tried to resolve the dilemma caused by the plunge in the pay standard coefficient when the PCE is substituted for the CPI, by using a third equation that includes as a price variable the ratio of housing costs to the PCE.[23]

In all, CWPS estimated nine equations, and even though each of these equations in the sensitivity analysis seems to have some advantages and disadvantages relative to the others, CWPS argued that its first specification was optimal and stuck to its assertion that the standards reduced wage inflation:

> The foregoing econometric results, based on conventional—indeed mainstream—pay and price equation specifications, provide convincing evidence that the pay standard had a modest but nonetheless significant effect on wage inflation. A best estimate is that the average annual rate of growth of hourly labor compensation was lowered by about 1 percentage point.[24]

The Importance of the Postcontrols Period

As indicated earlier, there is considerable evidence that it is important to account for the postcontrols period in assessing the impact of controls or guidelines.[25] Previously it was shown that the CWPS finding of a favorable impact of the standards on pay increases was highly sensitive to the precise assumptions and model specifications used. Here it will be shown that the same alleged program effects evaporate over time when a poststandards time period is added to the sample.

The first step in this analysis was to estimate wage equations similar to those used by both CWPS and GAO through the time period covered by their analyses.[26] Next, the same equations were used with

[23] All three of the equations cover the 1960-1980 period, because the PCE was developed in 1958. The results are somewhat mixed. On the one hand, CWPS found that its equation using the PCE is misspecified, and that the effect on pay rates of changes in home purchase prices and mortgage interest costs (omitted from the PCE) is indistinguishable from the effect of other components of the CPI. On the other hand, CWPS expressed surprise at the counterintuitive nature of the pattern of the coefficients of the twelve-quarter distributive lag on the ratio of housing costs to the PCE. The largest and only statistically significant coefficients are those on the far end of the lag—eight to twelve quarters—in contrast to the more expected patterns in the other equations.
[24] CWPS, *Evaluation of the Pay and Price Standards Program*, pp. 103-4.
[25] Blinder, *Economic Policy*; Ulman and Flanagan, *Wage Restraint*.
[26] Attempts to replicate the CWPS preferred basic pay equation yielded an equation very close but not identical to the CWPS equation. I used the same specification of the equation as CWPS and the same time frame, and attempted to measure the variables in the same way. The overall explanatory power of the two equations is identical (R^2s of 0.87), and the t-ratios for all variables are nearly the same, but the absolute size of the coefficients is different. In particular, I obtained a smaller but still statistically significant coefficient for the Carter standards dummy variable than did CWPS. In any event, my main point here is not to predict the precise size of any particular coefficient but to illustrate how sensitive the coefficient of a standards variable is to the addition of a few extra quarters of data beyond the expiration of the program.

TABLE 9
IMPACT OF WAGE-PRICE STANDARDS ON PAY RATES

	Coefficients and t-ratios of Standards Variable	
	Without post-standards period (1954-II – 1980-III)	With post-standards period (1954-II – 1981-III)
CWPS equation	−0.29 (−2.5)	−0.14 (−1.3)
GAO equation	−0.07 (−0.61)	0.03 (0.25)

NOTE: t-ratios are in parentheses.
SOURCE: From Meyer's equations replicating CWPS and GAO equations. The dependent variable is the BLS hourly earnings index multiplied by the ratio of total hourly compensation divided by hourly wages and salaries, as measured by the U.S. Department of Commerce. The full equations are shown in table 11.

TABLE 10
RESULTS OF THE PAY EQUATIONS OVER DIFFERENT TIME FRAMES

	1954-II – 1980-III		1954-II – 1981-III	
	Coefficient	t-ratios	Coefficient	t-ratios
Constant	0.85	18.08	0.89	19.09
Change in CPI (%)	3.59	6.93	3.65	6.34
Unemployment rate (%)[a]	−0.13	−6.01	−0.13	−5.85
Change in social security (%)	1.00	8.08	0.97	7.84
Change in minimum wage (%)	0.02	3.40	0.02	3.14
Kennedy-Johnson guideposts	−0.22	−3.73	−0.24	−3.88
ESP-I	0.11	1.08	0.13	1.28
ESP-II	−0.26	−2.24	−0.22	−1.84
Postcontrol period	0.04	0.25	0.14	0.97
Standards	−0.29	−2.47	−0.14	−1.32

NOTE: The dependent variable is the same as in table 10. $R^2 = 0.87$; F statistic $= 66.08$; D-W $= 2.05$.
[a]The unemployment rate is defined here as the difference between the actual unemployment rate for civilian workers and Robert Gordon's measure of the "natural" unemployment rate.
SOURCE: Equation estimated by Jack Meyer.

TABLE 11

RESULTS OF THE PAY EQUATION USING CHANGE IN
AVERAGE HOURLY EARNINGS INDEX
AS DEPENDENT VARIABLE, 1954-II – 1981-III

	Coefficient	t-ratios
Constant	0.85	18.44
Change in CPI (%)	3.54	5.97
Unemployment rate	−0.13	−5.88
Change in social security tax (%)	0.19	1.58
Change in minimum wage (%)	0.02	3.13
Kennedy-Johnson guideposts	−0.23	−3.72
ESP-I	0.10	0.98
ESP-II	−0.20	−1.69
Post-ESP control period	0.05	0.35
Standards	−0.15	−1.42

$R^2 = 0.84$
D-W = 2.02
SOURCE: Equation estimated by Jack Meyer.

the time period extended through the third quarter of 1981. This added one year to the CWPS sample period and one and a half years to the GAO sample period.

The results, summarized in table 9, support my contention that it is premature and misleading to assert that a set of standards has had an effect on wages or prices of a given magnitude prior to assessing the poststandards behavior of wages or prices. These results show that when one year of poststandards time is included (1980-III through 1981-III), the standards variable in the equation corresponding closely to the CWPS wage equation drops to *half* its former size. More important, when this equation is run through the poststandards period, the coefficient of the standards variable loses its statistical significance.

In the equation corresponding to the GAO work, of course, the standards impact was not significant in the first place.[27] When the longer time frame is used for this equation, the coefficient flips from negative and statistically insignificant to positive and statistically insignificant.

It is also noteworthy that in the first set of equations, the coefficient of the standards variable was the only one to switch from statisti

[27] This is because I used the GAO preferred equation that uses the PCE instead of the CPI as a measure of price changes.

cally significant to statistically insignificant or vice versa; indeed, most of the other *t*-ratios remained at about the same level when the subsequent four quarters of data were added, as shown in table 10.

Finally, to test the sensitivity of the results to the use of the measure of pay used by CWPS in its regression analyses (the hourly earnings index scaled up by a factor designed to account for employee benefits), I tested my equation for the 1954-II–1981-III period using simply the hourly earnings index as a dependent variable. The results were substantially the same as in my regular equation, with the size and statistical insignificance of the standards variable varying only very slightly from the results obtained using a variable reflecting total hourly compensation. (See table 11.)

In summary, the program impact on wages claimed by CWPS is shown to disappear when either an alternative measurement of a price variable or a postprogram period is included in the analysis. Contentions that the program had any impact on wages cannot be supported by a wage equation that is robust with regard to alternative, equally plausible specifications.

6
Incomes Policies over the Past Two Decades

To help place the preceding analysis in a historical context, this chapter provides a brief review of U.S. wage-price policies between 1960 and 1980. The Kennedy-Johnson guideposts, announced in 1962, were the first peacetime wage and price standards in the United States. Since then there have been two further peacetime incomes policies—the Nixon controls from 1971 to 1974 and the Carter wage-price standards during 1978–1980.

The Kennedy-Johnson Guideposts

The Kennedy guideposts, which emerged in 1962, were shaped to a considerable extent by the situation in the steel industry, an industry viewed by the government as a key source of price increases in a slack economy. A study by Otto Eckstein and Gary Fromm determined that steel prices had contributed considerably to inflationary pressures in the 1955–1958 period.[1] With rumors circulating that the steel industry would increase prices in late 1961 concurrently with increasing wages, and knowing that a major steel contract would expire in the summer of 1962, the administration concluded that it must prepare "general battle lines on the wage-price front."[2]

Maximum publicity accompanied the effort to discourage the steel industry from raising prices in 1961. Backed by the Council of Economic Advisers (CEA), several U.S. senators spoke on "the importance of stable steel prices and on the problems of concentration and price fixing in the industry."[3] To make it more appealing to the steel industry

---

This chapter was written by Patricia Samors.

[1] Otto Eckstein and Gary Fromm, *Steel and the Postwar Inflation*, Study Paper 2, prepared for the Joint Economic Committee, 86th Congress, 1st session, 1959.
[2] William J. Barber, "The Kennedy Years: Purposeful Pedagogy," in Craufurd D. Goodwin, ed., *Exhortation and Controls: The Search for a Wage-Price Policy 1945-1971* (Washington, D.C.: The Brookings Institution, 1975), p. 155.
[3] Ibid., p. 157.

to exercise restraint, President Kennedy made a statement at a press conference in August 1961 on the value of stable steel prices. Kennedy also directly addressed the leadership of the industry through a CEA-drafted letter arguing that the wage increment could be absorbed "by the advance in productivity"[4] within the industry and that a lack of price restraint could ultimately affect the industry negatively. The administration won this battle — prices were not increased in 1961— but it was still groping for a broad wage-price policy in late 1961 so that individual industries would not be singled out for "special" treatment. The guidelines were, therefore, shaped into a formula that would both accommodate the special problems of the steel industry and yet not be industry specific.

Before the guideposts were printed in the 1962 *Economic Report of the President*, however, they were used in the administration's campaign to induce restraint in the forthcoming 1962 collective-bargaining negotiations in the steel industry. The administration's objective was to avoid a steel price increase and wage-induced price increases in other industries where wage settlements and material costs were believed to be affected by the steel settlement.[5]

The administration hoped to achieve this objective by urging steel companies to follow its guidelines for wage behavior — linking the increase in wages to the lower of the industry or economy-wide increase in labor productivity. The labor contract emerging from the 1962 steel negotiations was consistent with the standards. In the Kennedy administration's view, a dual strategy had been launched: the steel contract was settled reasonably without any basis for price increases and a significant contribution was made in controlling the wage-price spiral by reducing the effect of wage-price changes in the steel industry on the rest of the economy.

The Johnson administration was also involved in several wage-price decisions. In 1964 it attempted to persuade the auto industry to cut prices before the upcoming wage negotiations and to keep the wage increases consistent with the guidelines. In 1965 the administration intervened in steel negotiations to obtain a noninflationary settlement. Finally, it persuaded Congress to enact a pay increase for civil service and postal employees within the guideposts.

The Kennedy-Johnson administrations promoted the guideposts by various means, including:

- numerous addresses to business, labor, and the public about the guideposts by members of CEA and of the cabinet, subcabinet officials, and the president

[4] Ibid., p. 158.
[5] Ibid., p. 166.

- an increased number of private communications and meetings between government officials and leaders of business and labor to emphasize the "public interest factor"
- formal statements by the Council of Economic Advisers to the public commenting on particular wage and price decisions (including statements on wage increases for employees of the New York Transit Authority, the five airlines involved in the July–August 1966 strike, the American Airlines case, and price increases for steel, aluminum, and copper)[6]

The Kennedy-Johnson guideposts were the least formal of the three peacetime incomes policies. The plan was based on the concept that inflation could be controlled if wage changes reflected productivity changes and price changes reflected only a pass-through of labor costs. The structure of the guideposts was focused on productivity growth because the administration viewed "the rapid advance of productivity" as "the key to the stability of the price level as money incomes rise."[7]

The Kennedy administration's original guide for noninflationary wage behavior declared that the rate of increase in hourly compensation (including both wages and employee benefits) in each industry should be equal to the trend rate of productivity increase for the economy as a whole, based on a five-year moving average. In the second phase of the program, during the Johnson administration, the wage increase was based on a 3.2 percent average annual change in output per man-hour. This rate had been identified as corresponding to the five-year moving average figure.

The general guide for noninflationary price behavior called for a reduction in prices if an industry's rate of productivity increase exceeded the rate of productivity increase for the economy as a whole. The premise underlying such a standard is that an industry with above-average productivity growth is likely to experience declining unit labor costs, as its high productivity growth would exceed the pace of wage increases. The guideposts provided for an appropriate increase in price if the reverse relationship prevailed, and for stable prices if the two rates of productivity increase were equal.

For the sake of efficiency and equity, however, there were exceptions and modifications to the rules. These alterations included varying the rate of wage increase depending on an industry's excess demand or surplus of labor and on the level of wages compared with those earned elsewhere by a similar work force. The rate of price

6 *Economic Report of the President*, Washington, D.C., 1967, pp. 125-29.
7 *Economic Report of the President*, 1962, p. 190.

increase was also allowed to deviate from the guideposts if an industry's level of profits was insufficient to attract the capital required to finance a needed expansion in capacity, if costs other than labor costs had fluctuated substantially, or if the relation of productive capacity to full employment demand suggested that an outflow of capital from the industry would be desirable. Comparison of profit rates with those earned elsewhere on investments of comparable risk was also a criterion used to permit modification of the price standards.

During the Kennedy and Johnson administrations, the guideposts appeared to work when there was relatively high unemployment and excess capacity and, thus, little upward pressure on prices. As the economy and inflation accelerated during the Vietnam War, however, business and labor officials began to ignore the guideposts. Settlements in the construction, airline, and metropolitan transit industries all broke the guidelines. To avoid serious embarrassment, the government unofficially dismantled the guideposts in 1967.

The Nixon Controls

On August 15, 1971, the Nixon administration placed a ninety-day freeze on all prices, rents, wages, and salaries, as part of its Economic Stabilization Program (ESP). After the freeze, called Phase I of the ESP, the government imposed three follow-up phases designed to ease the economy and the public away from mandatory controls. The Cost of Living Council (CLC), which was established to administer the freeze, continued to advise on further stabilization policies, actions, and goals in the later phases of the program. (For a general outline of the regulations in each phase, see the appendix.)

Phase II was intended from the outset to be a short-term incomes policy. The guidelines were quite comprehensive and mandatory, in principle, but there was a heavy reliance on self-administration. The Nixon administration was aiming for broad coverage but with limited governmental involvement. The Price Commission and the Pay Board had primary responsibility for developing the Phase II standards and made decisions on changes in prices and wages. In March 1972 the labor representatives on the Pay Board withdrew, and it was not until the Labor Management Advisory Committee was established in Phase III that labor once again participated in the ESP at a policy level.

Allowable wage increases in Phase II were based on the trend in productivity of the overall economy rather than on an industry-specific figure. Wage increases were permitted up to 5.5 percent (a standard that reflected the 3 percent productivity of the overall economy plus a residual inflation rate of 2 to 3 percent). Except for the largest employee units, wage increases up to 5.5 percent could be put in place without requiring prior notification or review, thus working toward the objective of self-administration. Exceptions were made for the correction of gross inequities and for workers whose pay had increased less than 7 percent a year for the past three years. In addition, workers earning less than $1.90 per hour were initially exempt. In July 1972 a court decision caused the CLC to raise the exemption threshold to exclude workers earning less than $2.75 per hour.[8]

The goal of maintaining largely self-administered controls also became a goal of the price standards. Price adjustments were allowed to compensate for cost increases as long as the rise in prices would not cause the firm's profit margin to exceed the margin of the best two of three fiscal years before the freeze. Because the firms themselves were to apply the rules on cost pass-through and profit margin, federal involvement in most price decisions was minimized. Again, all firms except the largest — those with annual sales above $100 million — could make the price adjustments without prenotification or approval.

The Phase II controls were relaxed in January 1973 for several reasons. First, the administration was hopeful that the participation of labor leadership in the program could be restored prior to the negotiation of several key labor agreements in 1973 (for example, Master Freight, rubber, and automobiles). Second, Phase III was meant to be a step toward a gradual removal of the controls. In Phase III "the government retained the enforcement ability and authority necessary to the nation's anti-inflation objective while leaving the private sector the maximum possible freedom to pursue productivity, efficiency and collective bargaining."[9] Third, the profit limitation rule was threatening business investment. And lastly, as economic activity increased during Phase II, the price ceilings, in an increasing number of cases, were impeding production and/or the efficient allocation of output. Thus, in Phase III, there was a shift by the administration to a more flexible program, a shift that some advocates of mandatory controls viewed as an unwarranted relaxation of the program.

During this phase, the Price Commission and the Pay Board were absorbed into the CLC, which assumed operational responsibility for the controls. The price standards were modified to reduce the constraint of the profit margin limitations by automatically permitting any price increases that did not exceed 1.5 percent. In addition, price adjustments were permitted, even if they exceeded the standards, if they were judged necessary to allocate resources efficiently or to maintain adequate levels of supply. Prenotification requirements were dis-

[8] Arnold R. Weber and Daniel J. B. Mitchell, *The Pay Board's Progress* (Washington, D.C.: The Brookings Institution, 1978), p. 76.
[9] *Economic Report of the President*, 1973, p. 82.

continued for wages and prices, although firms with sales over $250 million or more than 5,000 employees were required to provide quarterly reports to the CLC. The wage standard was similar to the one in Phase II, although there was an understanding that "no single standard for wage settlements can be equally applicable at one time to all parties."[10] This principle introduced more flexibility into the wage standard with respect to specific cases.

In December 1972, prices for food, especially meat, began to rise sharply. The big surge in food prices in 1973 was caused by strong consumer demand and a decline in the world supply. Ceilings on red-meat prices were imposed in March 1973 and in May prenotification requirements were reinstated, but by June food prices were still accelerating. Moreover, substantial price increases had become diffused throughout other sectors of the economy. The prevailing opinion that Phase III was a failure led to the termination of this phase and the imposition of the second freeze. This freeze covered only prices (except rent and raw agricultural products); wages were allowed to rise as under Phase III.

During July and August 1973, the freeze was lifted sector by sector and each sector was then placed under controls. It was the administration's intention to decontrol the economy subsequently on a sector-by-sector basis as well.

The objective of Phase IV was to develop a progressive program of decontrol that would ensure that the economy would move smoothly into a free-market system without a corresponding bulge of prices. The price regulations in Phase IV were similar to those in Phase II, although they were somewhat more stringent: costs could only be passed through on a dollar-for-dollar basis rather than on a percentage basis and prices in several sectors were limited to that portion of cost increases occurring since the last quarter of 1972 that was not reflected in prior price increases.[11] The wage increase limitations of Phase III were maintained in Phase IV. The pace of the decontrol process was gradual in 1973 but increased in early 1974 so that by April 30, 1974, only "12 percent of the CPI remained under control against 44 percent before decontrol began."[12]

The Interim Period

The Economic Stabilization Act of 1970 gave President Nixon the au-

[10] Marvin H. Kosters, *Controls and Inflation: The Economic Stabilization Program in Retrospect* (Washington, D.C.: The American Enterprise Institute, 1975), p. 23.
[11] Ibid., p. 25.
[12] Ibid., p. 27.

thority to initiate a program of wage and price controls. Yet, the consensus in Congress and among the American people at the end of April 1974 was that controls were not only destabilizing but also contributed to a stagnant economy. Therefore, it was not surprising that in March 1974 the Senate Banking, Housing, and Urban Affairs Committee unanimously voted against the Nixon administration's request to extend the Economic Stabilization Act. The extension would have allowed the Cost of Living Council to continue the process of decontrol, promote price stability through voluntary means, continue controls on the health care industry, and regulate prices of petroleum products. The committee's rejection of the proposal simply highlighted congressional feeling that controls were not the solution to the problems facing the economy in 1973 and early 1974 — namely, inflation and shortages.

In April and May 1974 the debate on inflation continued. The discussion centered on wage and price controls and the continuation of the Cost of Living Council, as described by Congressman Donald Riegle, with "the responsibility to study, monitor, and hopefully develop some recommendations about what can be done to stabilize prices."[13] Such an agency was deemed necessary to discover the sources of inflation and to develop measures to deal with them effectively.

On April 29, Senators Edmund Muskie, Adlai Stevenson, and J. Bennett Johnston submitted an amendment to a bill authorizing appropriations for the Council on International Economic Policy. This amendment was designed to enable the economy to shift smoothly from the existing system of wage and price controls to an uncontrolled free-market economy. In light of the high rate of inflation during this period, Senator Muskie felt that "Congress should not sit on its hands."[14] This amendment would have provided the president with the authority to monitor the economy and to enforce decontrol commitments. Moreover, it would have provided for wage and price control authority that was limited in nature and restricted to "a very narrow band of special circumstances in specific sectors of the economy."[15]

The debate in the Senate on April 29 and May 1 focused on a few key points: (1) the failure of the previous controls, (2) the administration's use of the controls, and (3) whether the existence of standby controls would discourage excessive wage and price increases. The amendment was split into two parts so that the monitoring authority

[13] Congressman Donald W. Riegle, Jr., *Congressional Record*, May 2, 1974, p. 12816.
[14] Senator Edmund S. Muskie, *Congressional Record*, April 29, 1974, p. 12203.
[15] Senator J. Bennett Johnston, Jr., *Congressional Record*, April 29, 1974, p. 12200.

would not be affected by a motion to table the standby control authority or vice versa. Provisions were adopted for the continuation of the CLC or a similar monitoring agency with the authority to enforce price restraint agreements while the standby control power was tabled. Senator Walter Mondale indicated that he simply could "not support issuing another blank check to this President."[16]

When consideration of the bill containing Muskie's amendment resumed on May 9, the senator indicated that there was a "clear need for the economic monitoring and decontrol" provisions.[17] The monitoring agency would "provide a distinct institutional force for Federal action on inflation"[18] and "evaluate the effect of a variety of Federal decisions on prices and availability of domestic products."[19] Furthermore, the agency would collect and analyze "economic data adequate to forecast special inflationary and shortage problems."[20] Data collected by the Bureau of Labor Statistics and the Commerce Department were only historical in nature, informing the public of the types of inflation and shortages experienced in the recent past, and they did not provide economic forecasts. Third, this anti-inflation agency would take action, excluding the use of controls, to avoid inflation and shortages—a need not filled by any other agency.

During the subsequent exchange, Senator John Tower introduced a substitute amendment which would have authorized an economic monitoring council. The council would "monitor the economy as a whole"[21] and enforce price restraint commitments, but its powers and staff would be limited to "avoid establishing a big bureaucracy that probably would be control oriented."[22] When Muskie urged the Senate to table the Tower amendment because it was "a shadow of what we need"[23] and his request was defeated, the Senate's sentiments on the two proposals were clear. Seeing that the Senate intended to drop his amendment in favor of a more limited monitoring proposal, and sensing that Tower's proposed council would be an ineffective monitoring authority without the resources to enforce the decontrol commitments, Senator Muskie moved to table the bill rather than vote on a proposal that would be an "illusory promise to the American people."[24] The motion passed.

[16] Senator Walter F. Mondale, *Congressional Record*, May 1, 1974, p. 12638.
[17] Senator Edmund S. Muskie, *Congressional Record*, May 9, 1974, p. 14099.
[18] Ibid.
[19] Ibid.
[20] Ibid.
[21] *Congressional Quarterly Almanac*, vol. 30, 93rd Congress, 2nd session, 1974 (Washington, D.C.; Congressional Quarterly Inc., 1975), p. 180.
[22] Ibid.
[23] Senator Edmund S. Muskie, *Congressional Record*, May 9, 1981, p. 14117.
[24] *Congressional Quarterly Almanac*, 1974, p. 180.

The other event in May 1974 that deserves attention was the appearance before the Senate Consumer Economic Subcommittee (of the Joint Economic Committee) of the former director of the Cost of Living Council, John T. Dunlop. At this hearing Dunlop expressed his belief that structural changes had to be created in the economy that would make it less vulnerable to inflation. This view provided the basis for his support of the administration's proposal for an inflation-monitoring agency. He was certain that this agency would provide a central focus within which the federal government and private-sector institutions could work "to explore, to stimulate and to induce necessary changes."[25] These activities would attempt to "get government and private groups to change their internal decision-making processes, their habits of mind and thought patterns, and their responses to their outside worlds."[26]

The discussion of controls and monitoring agencies was relatively quiet for the next several months. In early August, President Nixon sent a message to Congress in which he proposed the establishment of a cost of living task force. The president explained that although he continued to oppose mandatory controls, it was still essential that "wages and prices be carefully watched, that labor and management be constantly aware of public concern in this area, and that Government have the information it needs to persuade labor and management to do their duty"[27] to reduce inflation. This request was apparently put aside as the Watergate issue came to a head. Yet, three days after taking office, President Ford again raised the issue in his address to a joint session of Congress. The president, at this time, requested the authority to monitor wage and price increases in an "inflation-plagued" economy to expose abuses and inflationary price increases. He specifically asked that authority to impose controls not be granted.

Within the next few days the House and Senate Banking Committee held hearings on the request, reported the bill favorably, and sent it to the floor. The legislation represented a restricted approach to the problem of inflation by creating a cost of living task force, or as named by the Senate Committee, a Council on Wage and Price Stability. The bill did not include either mandatory or standby control authority. Roy Ash, director of the Office of Management and Budget (OMB), testifying before the House Committee, reported that the council would

[25] John T. Dunlop, "Inflation," Congressional Information Service, *Annual Abstracts*, 1975, J-841-8.1, p. 14.
[26] Ibid.
[27] Anti-Inflation Act of 1974, Report from the Committee on Banking and Currency, Report no. 93-1297, 93rd Congress, 2nd session, August 19, 1974, p. 1.

provide "the government the capability to work cooperatively with the private sector to identify areas that contribute to inflation."[28] More specifically, the council would "work with labor and management to improve the structure of collective bargaining," encourage price restraint, conduct public hearings to help publicize inflationary problems, "focus attention on the need to increase productivity," and "monitor the economy" by acquiring appropriate reports.[29]

On August 19 the bills went before the full House and Senate. In the debate on the House floor, the view was expressed that the monitoring authority was inadequate — "a cosmetic device to cover a lack of real and responsible action,"[30] and "far short of what really needs to be done."[31] Several Democrats, such as Congresswoman Leonor Sullivan and Congressman Henry Gonzalez, noted that the bill was "innocuous" and that the task force created "no moral authority that does not already exist."[32] Congressman John Rousselot opposed the bill, arguing that the federal government should monitor itself and that "by distracting attention from the real causes of inflation, monitoring will postpone the time when effective fiscal and monetary action is finally taken."[33] Despite these opinions, the majority of the House must have shared the view of Congressmen William Widnall and Robert Bauman that although the task force was "hardly a cure-all,"[34] it would "grant the President and the Congress a possible useful weapon in [the] joint effort to combat inflation,"[35] because the vote was well above the required two-thirds majority.[36]

As in the House, some members of the Senate were skeptical of the power embodied in the bill. Senator Adlai Stevenson noted that the bill had "no teeth."[37] Stevenson claimed that not only would the bill give the president no power to "require information on price or wage decisions" or to "restrain or defer excessive wage or price increases," but also it contained no subpoena provision "to strengthen the President's information gathering authority." In addition, he contended that it did not "provide adequate funding to do the job."[38]

Several amendments were proposed to address the bill's per-

[28] Ibid., p. 2.
[29] Ibid.
[30] Congressman John E. Moss, *Congressional Record*, August 19, 1974, p. 28949.
[31] Congressman Jonathan B. Bingham, *Congressional Record*, August 19, 1974, p. 28953.
[32] Congressman Henry B. Gonzalez, *Congressional Record*, August 19, 1974, p. 28950.
[33] Congressman John H. Rousselot, *Congressional Record*, August 19, 1974, p. 28955.
[34] Congressman William B. Widnall, *Congressional Record*, August 19, 1974, p. 28951.
[35] Congressman Robert E. Bauman, *Congressional Record*, August 19, 1974, p. 28957.
[36] A two-thirds majority was required because the House had suspended the rules to vote on the bill without the required three-day delay between the committee's report and House action.
[37] Senator Adlai E. Stevenson III, *Congressional Record*, August 19, 1974, p. 28885.
[38] Ibid.

ceived weaknesses, but they were ultimately defeated. These amendments would have provided authority for wage and price deferrals, information-gathering powers to provide in-depth analysis of inflation, and/or a budget of $5 million instead of the $1 million proposed. Furthermore, the council would have been empowered to disclose to federal law enforcement agencies and the public certain secret product-line profits if those profits were associated with inflationary price increases. The Senate did make two major changes in the bill, adopting an amendment by Senator Edward Kennedy terminating the council's authority on August 15, 1975, instead of June 30, 1975, and an amendment by Senator William Hathaway directing the council to look into the inflationary effect of "economic concentration and anti-competitive practices"[39] of both labor and industry. Despite the few misgivings, the members of the Senate were anxious to respond in good faith to the president's first legislative request and the bill passed 83–3.

The Senate's version of the bill was accepted by the House on August 20, 1974, by a vote of 369–27. Thus, only a few months after refusing President Nixon's request to extend the Cost of Living Council's authority to perform the same functions, the Congress cleared the way for another federal inflation-monitoring agency, the Council on Wage and Price Stability, by an overwhelming majority.

The Carter Guidelines

The next set of wage-price guidelines was introduced informally in January 1978. At that time President Carter stated that "every effort should be made to reduce the rate of wage and price increase in 1978 to below the average rate of the past two years."[40] Each company was asked to hold its wage and price increases in 1978 significantly below the average annual rate for the preceding two years. This initial "deceleration" program provided only industry targets; there were no rules for wage and price decisions within individual firms.

In October 1978 the Carter administration announced more explicit wage-price standards as part of a more comprehensive anti-inflation program. The new wage-price program was intended to be a voluntary effort, with the Council on Wage and Price Stability performing a formal review of average wage and price increases for employee units and product lines. In initiating this new program Carter

---

[39] *Congressional Quarterly Almanac*, p. 181.
[40] Robert W. Hartman, "The Budget and the Economy," in Joseph A. Pechman, ed., *Setting National Priorities: The 1979 Budget* (Washington, D.C.: The Brookings Institution, 1978), p. 56.

was not required to establish a new enforcement agency, as was Nixon; instead, he simply broadened the scope and responsibilities of CWPS, which was already in existence. Public opinion, business goodwill, and the threat of the loss of government contracts were intended to be used as tools to encourage labor and management to comply with the standards. Even though the standards were allegedly voluntary, CWPS filled the *Federal Register* with rules for appropriate behavior that were difficult to distinguish from regulations. In addition, larger companies were requested to send in reports to the council, a procedure also followed under mandatory controls.

In the first year of the program, the pay standard limited hourly wages and private fringe benefit increases to a maximum of 7 percent for each employee group in a company. In the second year, the allowable pay increase was raised to between 7.5 and 9.5 percent. Exempt from the pay standards were workers who earned an hourly wage below a certain rate (originally $4 per hour), an employee group that was in a close tandem relationship with another, job categories in which there were acute labor shortages, and wage increases in excess of the standard that were offset by productivity-improving changes in work practices.

The Carter price standard was designed to accommodate the variations in rates of price increase from industry to industry. Yet the administration regarded a variable price standard based upon a pass-through of costs as inappropriate because this was believed to reduce the incentive to cut costs. The administration felt that its price standard addressed these two problem areas by requiring average prices to increase at a rate of at least 0.5 percentage points less than the firm's average price increase during 1976–1977 (but no more than 9.5 percent). Price increases of less than 1.5 percent were also permitted. During the second year, an additional 1 percent increase in the basic price standard was allowed. In those cases where a firm could not calculate an average price for its products or where it experienced uncontrollable cost increases, an alternative profit-margin standard was available. Approximately one-third of all companies used this alternative. In addition, companies in wholesale and retail trade and food manufacturing and processing were allowed to use a special percentage margin standard. This standard covered another one-fourth of all companies. According to a CWPS evaluation, about one-third of all companies actually followed the regular price standard.[41]

Carter's wage and price program ended after two years for several reasons. First, inflation had persisted at double-digit rates throughout

[41] CWPS, *Evaluation of the Pay and Price Standards Program,* January 16, 1981, p. 28.

the program. Second, workers and firms appeared unwilling to moderate wage and price rises in the expectation that the program would restrain inflation. Third, support for the standards diminished when they were perceived as being "bent" in a few large union settlements. Finally, there was a growing problem of wage-rate inequities because of the indexing of some wage rates to price inflation.[42]

[42] Barry P. Bosworth, "Economic Policy," in Joseph A. Pechman, ed., *Setting National Priorities: Agenda for the 1980s* (Washington, D.C.: The Brookings Institution, 1980), p. 63.

7
Conclusion

There is no solid evidence that President Carter's 1978–1980 wage-price guidelines had any effect on the pace of wage and price inflation. Administration claims of a program impact on wages have been shown to be largely illusory. Estimates of the program's impact on wages are highly sensitive to the exact specification of a wage equation, as well as to the precise time period studied. The Council on Wage and Price Stability found an apparent small though statistically significant program impact on wages under one of many alternative specifications. This impact is shown to evaporate, however, either when different but equally plausible specifications of a wage equation are estimated or when wage trends during an additional year beyond the program are taken into account. My findings show that the same catch-up phenomenon found in previous incomes policies both in the United States and abroad also characterized the period following the Carter guidelines.

In my view, the Carter guidelines were intended as a self-standing anti-inflation program, to be coupled with some fairly weak efforts toward fiscal restraint. When this strategy was quickly discredited by a policy and financial community demanding real fiscal and monetary restraint, the Carter administration shifted gears and accepted tacitly the higher interest rates and unemployment associated with real belt-tightening. Yet it left the apparatus of the guidelines intact and, I believe, went through the motions of running a wage-price program that, in effect, had been thrown over at the outset. This is not to question in any way the sincerity or commitment of those people who designed and ran the CWPS program. They attempted to devise and implement an internally consistent program. Yet the program seemed to be cut adrift from the administration's overall economic policy. There was hardly any mention of the program or use of its enforcement mechanisms by anyone outside of CWPS.

Perhaps there would have been a more significant program impact had President Carter expressed the degree of interest in his incomes policy that President Johnson expressed over his own guideposts. Perhaps it would not have made much difference. Indeed, there is little indication that any of these programs in the United States or abroad have much lasting impact on inflation, no matter how actively they are pursued. The gap between the elaborate detail of the Carter program design, however, and the apparent lack of interest in it at the White House damaged the credibility of the Carter administration's economic policy. Its credibility was further damaged by the disparity between the administration's commitment to deregulation in a few selected industries (a commitment that produced some very useful results) and its sponsorship of a program that was, in one sense, the ultimate regulatory scheme, blanketing the economy with a detailed set of rules, regulations, exceptions, and appeals processes covering millions of wages and prices.

Despite my serious misgivings about the guidelines, it was disappointing to see CWPS abolished. The activities of CWPS described in chapter 2 had some value, and a small, independent agency conducting selected reviews of collective bargaining, industry price behavior, and government regulation would have been a low-cost, worthwhile unit to keep intact.

In my view, using existing large-scale government agencies to fulfill these functions is less efficient and less useful than having a small, nonbureaucratic group monitor cost-increasing behavior and suggest policies for improving the efficiency of the economy. Fears of such an agency mandating controls in a strict or a de facto sense could be addressed by means of more restrictive legislation prohibiting such activity.

Ultimately, we must seek lasting solutions to the problem of inflation, and these will not emerge from the activities of a group like CWPS or its predecessors. Such a course requires the steady withdrawal of the excessive government stimulus to the economy in a credible fashion. Nevertheless, a small independent monitoring unit could serve to balance the more macroeconomic focus of the Council of Economic Advisers by concentrating on microeconomic aspects of the problem of inflation. Such an agency could foster at least marginal improvements in economic efficiency that would probably easily justify its cost.

Appendix
The Nixon Wage-Price Controls

REGULATIONS UNDER PHASES II, III, AND IV OF THE NIXON PROGRAM

Program	Phase II (Nov. 14, 1971, to Jan. 11, 1973)	Phase III (Jan. 11, 1973, to June 13, 1973)	Phase IV (Aug. 12, 1973, to date)
		General Standards	
Price increase limitations	Percentage pass-through of allowable cost increases since last price increase, or January 1, 1971, adjusted for productivity and volume offsets. Term limit pricing option available.	Self-administered standards of Phase II.	In most manufacturing and service industries dollar-for-dollar pass-through of allowable cost increases since last fiscal quarter ending prior to January 11, 1973.
Profit margin limitations	Not to exceed margins of the best two of three fiscal years before August 15, 1971. Not applicable if prices were not increased above base level or if firms "purified" themselves.	Not to exceed margins of the best two fiscal years completed after August 15, 1968. No limitation if average price increase does not exceed 1.5 percent.	Same years as for Phase III except that a firm that had not charged a price for any item above its base price, or adjusted freeze price, whichever is higher, was not subject to the limitation.
Wage increase limitations	General standard of 5.5 percent. Exceptions made to correct gross inequities and for workers whose pay had increased less than 7 percent a year for the past 3 years. Workers earning less than $2.75 per hour were exempt. Increases in qualified fringe benefits were permitted, raising standard to 6.2 percent.	General Phase II standard, self-administered. Some special limitations. More flexibility with respect to specific cases. Workers earning less than $3.50 per hour were exempted after May 1.	Self-administered standards or Phase III. Executive compensation limited.

Prenotification

Prices	Prenotification required for all firms with annual sales above $100 million, thirty days before implementation, approval required.	After May 2, 1973, prenotification required for all firms with sales above $250 million whose price increases have exceeded a weighted average of 1.5 percent.	Same as Phase II except that prenotified price increases may be implemented in thirty days unless CLC requires otherwise.
Wages	Prenotification required for all increases of wages for units of 5,000 or more workers, and for all increases above the standard regardless of the number of workers involved.	None required.	None required.

Reporting

Prices	Quarterly for firms with sales over $50 million.	Quarterly for firms with sales over $250 million.	Quarterly for firms with sales over $50 million.
Wages	Pay adjustments below standard for units having more than 1,000 persons.	Pay adjustments for units having more than 5,000 persons.	As in Phase III.
Special areas	Health, insurance, rent, construction, public utilities.	Health, food, public utilities, construction, petroleum.	Health, food, petroleum, construction, insurance, executive and variable compensation.
Exemptions to price standards	Raw agricultural commodities, import prices, export prices, firms with sixty or fewer employees.	Same as Phase II, plus rents.	Same as Phase II, plus manufactured feeds, cement, public utilities, lumber, copper scrap, long-term coal contracts, automobiles, fertilizers, nonferrous metals except aluminum and copper, mobile homes, and conductors.

SOURCE: Cost of Living Council (CLC).

Selected AEI Publications

AEI Associates Program

Wage-Price Standards and Economic Policy

JACK A. MEYER

This study assesses the wage-price policy pursued by the U.S. Council on Wage and Price Stability during its six-year existence, from 1974 to 1980. Focusing primarily on the wage-price standards introduced by President Carter in 1978, it evaluates their effect on wage and price trends during the two years they were in force.

The author argues that President Carter's guidelines were intended to be the centerpiece of the administration's anti-inflation program, but they were discredited at the outset. Instead of being abandoned, however, the guidelines remained in place for two years, with limited support from the public and from the administration itself.

The study also views the Carter wage-price standards as a case study of government regulation, highlighting the contradiction between the administration's commitment to reduce government regulation and its introduction of a program that would regulate millions of wage and price decisions. Criteria for defining the scope of a wage-price program are discussed, and the effectiveness of the wage-price standards assessed. By reporting and interpreting the results of a sensitivity analysis, the author questions claims that the guidelines had noticeably slowed the pace of wage increases.

The author, former assistant director for wage-price monitoring of the U.S. Council on Wage and Price Stability, is resident fellow in economics and director of health policy research at the American Enterprise Institute.

ISBN 0-8447-3490-X

 American Enterprise Institute for Public Policy Research
1150 Seventeenth Street, N.W., Washington, D.C. 20036